1000 ARTIST TRADING CARDS

GLOUCESTER MASSACHUSETTS

1000 ARTIST TRADING CARDS

INNOVATIVE AND INSPIRED
MIXED-MEDIA ATCs

QUARRY BOOKS

PATRICIA BOLTON

EDITOR-IN-CHIEF OF *CLOTH PAPER SCISSORS* AND *QUILTING ARTS MAGAZINE*

First published in the United States of America by
Quarry Books, a member of
Quayside Publishing Group
33 Commercial Street
Gloucester, Massachusetts 01930-5089
Telephone: (978) 282-9590
Fax: (978) 283-2742
www.quarrybooks.com

Library of Congress Cataloging-in-Publication Data
Bolton, Patricia.
    1,000 artist trading cards : innovative and inspired mixed media ATCs / Patricia Bolton.
        p.   cm.
    Includes index.
    ISBN 1-59253-334-5 (pbk.)
    1. Miniature craft. 2. Trading cards. I. Title. II. Title: One thousand artist trading cards.
    TT178.B65 2007
    760—dc22   2006026685
                                                          CIP

ISBN-13: 978-1-59253-334-3
ISBN-10: 1-59253-334-5

10 9 8 7 6 5 4 3 2

Design: Laura H. Couallier, Laura Herrmann Design
Cover Image and Photography: Allan Penn

Printed in China

OPPOSITE

0898	Kerrie Guinane
0084	Jean K. Brown
0497	Emmy Geppert
0199	Juanita Olson
0254	Christina Nelson
0828	Joanna van Ritbergen

0977   0692   0186

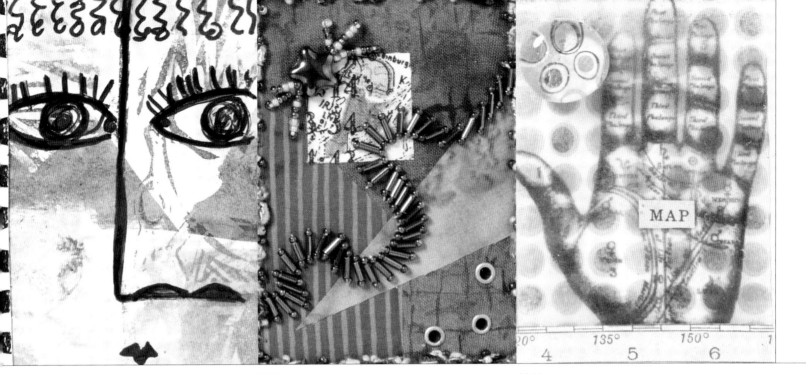

0840   0600   0340

CONTENTS

INTRODUCTION

0774

THEY'RE EVERYWHERE. They are traded at mixed-media retreats, trafficked through quilt shows and guild meetings, swapped at lectures, handed out at collage classes, exchanged through the Internet—any place mixed-media, fabric, and collage artists have the opportunity to meet, deals are going down. Fast, fun, and often frivolous, they are artist trading cards, otherwise known as ATCs. ATCs are little 2.5" × 3.5" (6.4 × 8.9 cm) pieces of art—mini-collages of fiber or paper (or both)—that an artist makes and trades with someone else. The artwork appears on one side, while the back side typically contains the artist's information including name, date the ATC was made, number in a series, and email address so the recipient can contact the artist with any questions or comments about the ATC's construction. There are no rules in creating ATCs except for the 2.5" × 3.5" (6.4 × 8.9 cm) size. Anything goes for composition and embellishment: fabric, paper, yarn, metal, found objects, and collage images are just a few items often found on ATCs.

A couple of years ago, fiber artist Janet Ghio wrote an article introducing fabric ATCs to our *Quilting Arts Magazine* audience. The article was extremely well received, and because our editorial team relishes hosting reader challenges, we thought it would be great fun to host a swap between our readers and our *Quilting Arts* staff. Little were we prepared for the reception of the challenge: When it closed, we received an overwhelming 800 fabric ATCs. Astounding! Since that challenge, we've hosted a couple of other ATC trades through our sister publication *Cloth Paper Scissors* as well as the Editor's Blog, with similar success.

0888

0095

An ATC is a fantastic little platform on which to try new techniques or experiment with different media without the pressures of creating a masterpiece. Have you never worked with fabric? Want to try your hand at collage? Using ATCs to explore an art form or technique can increase your arsenal of artistic skills, and, by trading them, provide you with great exposure to new artistic styles, techniques, media, ideas, and genres. If you're looking for the ATC to serve a purpose beyond creating, experimenting, and trading, you can also use them as business cards to promote your art.

If you have experienced a stall in your own creative endeavors and need a boost or want to get some ideas for creating ATCs, look no further than this book. Here you'll find an impressive gallery of 1,000 mixed-media ATCs submitted by readers of *Cloth Paper Scissors* and *Quilting Arts Magazine*. Many different art forms, media, and styles can be found in the pages ahead. If you've never made ATCs or are hoping to learn a few collage and fabric techniques, you'll also find some of my favorite mixed-media ATC projects. ENJOY!

Yours in creativity,
Patricia Bolton
Editor-in-Chief
Quilting Arts Magazine
and *Cloth Paper Scissors*

0774   j.m.scioli
0095   Valerie Lasure
0888   Sidney S. Inch

BASICS

IDEAS AND PROJECTS FOR CREATING INNOVATIVE MIXED-MEDIA ATCs

I hope you're not merely amazed by the ingenuity and beauty of the ATCs in this book, but are also inspired to try your hand at making your own. If you've never created ATCs before, get ready for a delightful artistic journey. As you can see in this book, there are no rules or limits for embellishment, just a couple of points you need to know before you get started.

* Your finished ATC should measure 2.5" × 3.5" (6.4 × 8.9 cm) in size.

* The back of your ATC should include your name, the date you created the ATC, its number in a series (if it's part of a series), and your email address or other contact information if you'd like the recipient to contact you about the ATC.

TOOLKIT FOR MIXED-MEDIA ATCs

There are a few gadgets and embellishments I recommend having on hand for creating fabric and paper ATCs. Don't worry if you don't have many of these items; some of the cleverest ATCs are those made simply from a mixture of found objects and wit.

* 9" × 12" (22.9 × 30.5 cm) sheets of black synthetic felt by Kunin
Available in most craft stores, felt provides a solid yet supple foundation for both paper and fabric ATCs. Synthetic felt consists of an acrylic/polyester blend of fibers, and it distorts when extreme, concentrated heat, such as that from a heat gun, is applied—ideal for creating burned effects. (Natural wool felt does not burn.)

* 90-lb. hot or cold press watercolor paper

* white tissue paper

* decorative tissue papers and gift-wrap papers

* sheets with collage images
These can be found in craft stores, on eBay, and from a variety of Internet-based stores.

* scrapbook paper

* fabric scraps of every kind

* PVA glue

* glue sticks

* **gel matte medium**

  I use Golden gel medium to glue items for collage and to transfer images from a transparency to a paper or fabric background.

* **fusible webbing**

  WonderUnder is a fusible webbing of glue backed on nonstick "release" paper traditionally used to fuse fabrics. (It also works with paper.) The fusible webbing melts and adheres to the fabric when heat is applied from an iron. When it has cooled, the release paper is pulled away, leaving the fusible glue on the fabric. WonderUnder comes on a bolt and is available at fabric, quilting, and many major craft stores.

  I typically make a batch of several ATCs from a collaged background I've created and then fused to the 9" × 12" (22.9 × 30.5cm) sheets of craft felt. A rotary cutter, mat, and quilting ruler make the job of cutting the sheets into individual ATCs quick and easy.

* **set of fine-tipped markers in different colors**

  Pigma pens are wonderful; they use waterproof archival ink, are perfect for writing on fabric and paper, and help to color in open areas on ATCs.

* **coloring agents to color fabric and paper**

  Keep a variety of coloring agents on hand, but if you're just getting started and/or have a limited budget, start with a watercolor set, Lumiere paints, and some Golden acrylic glazes, including those in the quinacridone family, which have a warm, yellow-gold quality in the undertone and are lightfast.

* **small rubberstamp alphabet and number set**

* **rubberstamps with abstract imagery, quotes, and figures**

* **black ink rubberstamp pad**

* **decorative trims, yarns, and ribbons**

* **embellishments of every kind**

  You probably have more of an embellishment stash on hand than you realize: buttons from discarded shirts, those seed beads and charms from that bead project you may not have finished, glass pebbles, old wooden letters and motifs, and so on. You'll never look at anything at a garage sale, flea market, or on eBay the same way again!

* **pair of fabric scissors and pair of paper scissors**

* **rotary cutter, rotary mat, and quilt ruler**

* **set of inexpensive paintbrushes in various sizes and shapes**

* **1" (2.5 cm) foam brushes**

* **cosmetic wedges**

  Cosmetic wedges are an inexpensive and effective way to smear paint, glue, and gel medium around a canvas.

* spray bottle

* iron and ironing board

* heat gun

* sewing machine and threads and/or hand threads and stitching needles

  Chenille and tapestry needles work splendidly if you choose to hand stitch instead.

For the more adventuresome, I'd also recommend:

* Bo-Nash 007 Bonding Agent

  Bo-Nash consists of saltlike crystals of fusible webbing you can sprinkle sparsely or liberally to fuse fabrics and fibers to your artwork.

* nylon chiffon scarves

  These work well for sandwiching fibers, bonding, and burning.

* craft metal

* various silk fibers and papers

* eyelets and eye-setting tool

* water-soluble oil pastels

* fabric paints including metallic paints

* set of Shiva Paintstiks

  These are highly pigmented oil sticks loaded with vibrant color that can be used on fabric.

* embossing powders and pigment inkpads

* glitter

* soldering iron or versatile heat and burning tool

  I use the Creative Textile Tool by Walnut Hollow.

* stencils

* Hot-Fix Angelina fibers

  Hot-fix Angelina fibers are glossy, synthetic, hairlike fibers that melt and fuse when heat is applied. Angelina fibers come in a wide variety of iridescent colors and can be stitched, fused with other fibers using a fusible webbing, or impressed with a rubberstamp and a warm iron to create an embossed design.

* Three-dimensional paints

  Puff Paint and Xpandaprint are two brands to use. Three-dimensional paints expand and bubble when concentrated heat is applied.

To create quirky and whimsical ATCs, be on the lookout for:

* quotes from fortune cookies

* small embellishments and ephemera

  Watch parts, small keys, shells, vintage postage stamps, buttons, etc.

* interesting designs and motifs

  Found in scrapbook papers and fabrics.

PROJECT 1

COLLAGED FELT ATCS FOR STITCHING

There are hoards of striking tissue papers, gift-wrap papers, and scrapbook papers that would be terrific to collage and stitch, but how do you keep them from tearing? In *Cloth Paper Scissors*, mixed-media artist Beryl Taylor shared her process of adhering papers to a cotton muslin base to create a new fabric suitable for stitching. I've adapted her technique, instead choosing to work with felt, fusible webbing, and gel medium. For these small ATCs, felt provides a slightly thicker foundation, making it easier to grab and manipulate as the ATC passes through your sewing machine (if you choose to stitch).

MATERIALS

- 9" × 12" (22.9 × 30.5 cm) sheet of felt

- torn bits of scrapbook papers

- decorative tissue papers (sewing patterns or gift wrap tissue with floral designs or writing are my favorites)

- 9" × 12" (22.9 × 30.5 cm) piece of fusible webbing (such as WonderUnder)

- 9" × 12" (22.9 × 30.5 cm) piece of white tissue paper

- acrylic gel medium (regular matte)

- coloring agents of choice (I use watercolor paints, fluid acrylics, water-soluble crayons, oil pastels, and Tim Holtz "Distress" inkpads)

- black rubberstamping ink (Stāz-On ink is recommended; it dries instantly.)

- rubberstamps and/or stencils (I choose designs with text and/or abstract imagery)

- acrylic glaze in yellow (such as Golden Quinacridone Nickel Azo Gold)

- embellishments (beads, buttons, ephemera)

- metallic paints (such as Lumiere)

- iron

- heat gun

- rotary cutter, ruler, and rotary mat

- sewing machine and threads

CREATING THE COLLAGED BACKGROUND

1   Set your iron to the cotton setting and, following the manufacturer's instructions, iron the fusible webbing to the felt. When cool, peel off the paper backing.

2   Fuse the 9" × 12" (22.9 × 30.5 cm) piece of white tissue paper to the fusible webbing side of the felt piece.

3   Tear bits of scrapbook papers and cover the white tissue paper with them using gel medium as your glue. Go ahead and slather the gel medium onto each piece. (The gel medium that seeps through the edges of the scrapbook papers will act as a resist when it comes time to color.) *(See Sample 1)*

4   Tear bits of decorative tissue papers and sewing patterns and place on top of the scrapbook papers for a more complex look.

Juxtaposing floral designs and straight, architectural lines from the sewing patterns will produce depth and interest. *(See Sample 2)*

5   Take your black rubberstamping ink and favorite rubberstamps and randomly stamp all over the collaged felt.

COLORING THE BACKGROUND

1   Now for the fun part: Take your coloring agents, such as watercolors, and paint the background. Let the colors run into one another. When dry, take either yellow fluid acrylic or Golden's Quinacridone Nickel Azo Gold and paint in various areas on top. The resulting rich mix of colors will delight you. *(See Sample 3)*

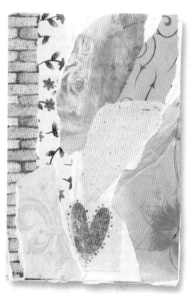

SAMPLE 1

SAMPLE 2

SAMPLE 3

2 Heat-set with a heat gun.

3 If you want an even more complex background, take some acrylic or metallic paint and randomly add stenciled or stamped designs.

CUTTING YOUR ATCS

1 Lay your piece of collaged felt onto a quilting mat.

2 Measure 2.5" (6.4 cm) -width increments across the collaged felt and cut with your rotary cutter.

3 Turning to the side of the mat so you can cut crosswise, measure 3.5" (8.9 cm) -length increments. Cut. Usually the felt will yield 8 to 9 ATCs, depending on how you orient the cutting.

EMBELLISHMENT

Now your ATCs are ready for stitch and embellishment—the options are limitless! You can:

✱ Rubberstamp images on hand-dyed fabric, cut out, then machine stitch on top of the collaged felt.

✱ Cut geometric shapes from fabrics and stitch to the ATC for an abstract design.

✱ Accent the background elements with free-motion stitching and beading.

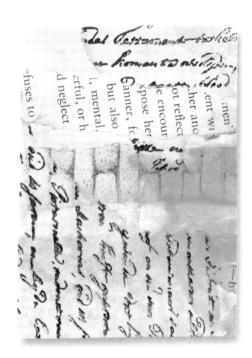

PROJECT 2

COLORFUL
FABRIC ATCS

MATERIALS

- 9" × 12" (22.9 × 30.5 cm) piece of black-and-white fabric

- coloring agents
  (I use Tsukineko all-purpose inks and watered-down Golden acrylic glazes)

- 9" × 12" (22.9 × 30.5 cm) piece of felt or batting for the back

- fusible webbing
  (such as WonderUnder)

- masking tape

- paintbrushes

- spray bottle

- cup of water

- roll of paper towels

- heat gun

- plastic wrap to protect your table surface

- sewing machine and threads

Rummage around the Internet and you might find some black-and-white upholstery fabrics that have interesting designs but are crying out for a little color. While surfing eBay, I stumbled across 30 yards (27 m) of a black-and-white upholstery fabric with a king and queen theme. I bought the lot for just $45. (What a steal!) I've been having a lot fun painting this fabric with inks, paints, and watercolors and cutting out the designs to place on my ATCs. Unlike traditional methods of fabric painting and dyeing in which the fabric needs to be washed in a solution to make the paint and dye permanent, I do not worry about this step because these newly colored fabrics will never be washed.

1 Tape plastic wrap with masking tape to your table surface.

2 Place the fabric on top of the plastic wrap.

3 Take your spray bottle and lightly mist the fabric. This will help the colors move and blend into one another as you paint.

4 Dip your paintbrush in a color of choice and simply begin to paint an area. Take another color and paint some more, overlapping the first color in certain areas. Don't worry if the paint is dark and obscuring the fabric design; when the color dries it will lighten significantly. If you're still concerned, however, you can use a paper towel to blot the fabric. (You'll also have created a beautiful, colorful paper towel that you can later use for collage.)

5 When you have completely painted your fabric, allow it to dry. You can also apply a heat gun to the fabric if you'd like to speed up the drying process.

USING YOUR NEWLY PAINTED FABRIC IN AN ATC

You can either use the fabric as a background for your ATC or cut out various designs or motifs in the fabric to use as focal points.

BACKGROUND FABRIC

1 Using fusible webbing, fuse the 9" × 12" (22.9 × 30.5 cm) piece of fabric to a piece of 9" × 12" (22.9 × 30.5 cm) felt or batting.

2 With your ruler, rotary cutter, and rotary mat, measure and cut the fabric into 2.5" × 3.5" (6.4 × 8.9 cm) pieces. (You should be able to get approximately 8 or 9 ATCs from the 9" × 12" [22.9 × 30.5 cm] sheet, depending on how you orient the cutting.)

3 Embellish the ATCs as desired.

For this ATC, I used the newly colored fabric as a background, then stamped Stamper's Anonymous "Wordsy Woman" with black ink on another piece of hand-dyed yellow fabric. I cut out the stamped fabric and glued it to the background with fabric glue. I embellished her top with three small, pink mother-of-pearl buttons, added a scrap of numbered fabric down the right side, and then zigzag-stitched the border.

FABRIC MOTIFS AS FOCAL POINTS

In these four examples, the king and queen images are used as focal points and fashioned into faux, embellished playing cards.

1 Cut out the portion of the fabric you'd like to use as a focal point for your ATC.

2 Choose a contrasting background for your ATC. I often use black and white fabric as it lends a sense of whimsy and contrast to the newly colored fabric.

3 Zigzag- or straight-stitch your design to the background fabric.

4 Embellish as desired.

In the king and queen examples, I cut out the images of royalty, then stamped small rubberstamps of hearts, diamonds, clubs, and spades on hand-dyed fabric. I zigzag-stitched the kings and queens to black-and-white fabric, appliquéd the various smaller designs in two corners, then satin-stitched the borders. For embellishment, I used bonded Swarovski crystals on the queens and hand stitching for the kings' garments.

PROJECT 3
SHIMMERING ATCS

MATERIALS

- small scraps of synthetic fabrics, each about 1" (2.5 cm) square or less in size (It's important that these fabrics consist of synthetic fibers, not natural fabrics; otherwise the fabrics won't burn the way you want them to.)

- 4" × 6" (10.2 × 15.2 cm) piece of sheer polyester chiffon

- 4" × 6" (10.2 × 15.2 cm) piece of wool felt for the base layer (Make sure this is a natural wool felt rather than a synthetic such as Kunin, Pellon, or Timtex—you don't want this bottom layer to burn.)

- stencil design of choice (In this example I used a fleur-de-lis pattern I'd cut from a scrapbook paper.)

- optional: gilding medium (such as Treasure Gold) or Shiva Paintstik in a metallic gold color

- fine-tip waterproof felt marker (such as Pigma pens)

- sewing machine

- machine threads

- sewing pins

- soldering iron with a fine-point tip

- ruler

- fabric scissors

SAFETY TIP:

It is essential to take safety precautions whenever you are using a heat gun or soldering iron. Make certain to work outside or in a well-ventilated area so you do not inhale potentially toxic fumes.

Creating these ATCs will dazzle you as you burn away top layers of sheer fabrics to reveal luminous colors below. This process involves taking synthetic fabrics and melting them with a fine-tipped soldering iron. I was first introduced to this particular fabric burning method by Fay Maxwell in her article for *Quilting Arts Magazine*, but have adapted it to include a central fleur-de-lis motif for an ATC.

1   Randomly place your scraps of synthetic fabrics on top of the felt base. Go ahead and layer them on top of one another, making sure to completely cover the felt. The more layers you have, the richer your resulting fabric will be.

2   Once you've completely covered the felt base with layers of fabric scraps, place the 4" × 6" (10.2 × 15.2 cm) piece of polyester chiffon fabric on top to trap the fabrics. Pin together to keep the layers in place. With your ruler, measure the ATC size in the center. Mark the border with your waterproof marker.

3   Center your stencil in the middle of the ATC and trace around the outline of the stencil. *(Sample 1)*

4   Carefully take your fabric sandwich to your sewing machine and straight-stitch the border of the ATC. Remove the pins.

5   Machine-stitch around your stenciled design.

6   Machine-stitch the ATC in a gridlike pattern around the motif. *(Sample 2)*

7   Cut the ATC to size with your fabric scissors.

8   Satin-stitch the border.

9   Turn on your soldering iron. When it is hot (this usually takes about five minutes), carefully burn out the stenciled design and the squares created by the machine-stitched grids. The longer you apply the soldering iron to an area, the more it will burn, so be careful.

10 When you are satisfied with the burned design, you can give the stenciled design a higher contrast. Gild it with some Treasure Gold or Shiva Paintstik.

This sample shows the sandwich of felt, fiber scraps, and a top layer of chiffon fabric. The ATC border and fleur-de-lis have been marked with a fine-tipped felt pen for machine embroidery. (NOTE: Sewing pins were removed for this photo so the design could be viewed more easily.)

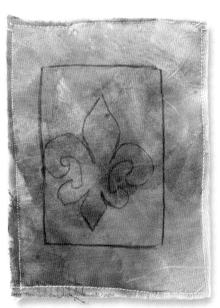

SAMPLE 1

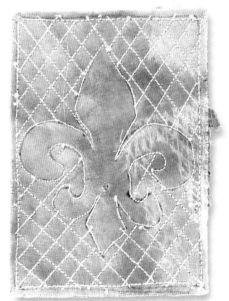

SAMPLE 2

PROJECT 4

FABRIC ATCS
BONDED WITH
THREAD SNIPPETS

- 9" × 12" (22.9 × 30.5 cm) piece of black felt

- 9" × 12" (22.9 × 30.5 cm) piece of hand-dyed fabric

- metallic fabric paint

- stamp pad

- fabric glue

- foiling glue

- 9" × 12" (22.9 × 30.5 cm) piece of fusible webbing (such as WonderUnder)

- chiffon scarf

- funky yarns, threads, cheesecloth, and bits of metal

- variegated threads

- tiny snippets of fusible webbing or Bo-Nash 007 Bonding Agent

- 2 to 3 rubberstamps with simple, abstract imagery and/or text

- two 1" (2.5 cm) foam brushes

- sheets of foil

- bone folder

- scissors

- 14" × 14" (35.6 × 35.6 cm) piece of parchment paper

- iron and ironing board

- sewing machine with free-motion capabilities

- heat gun

- rotary cutter, quilting ruler, and quilting mat

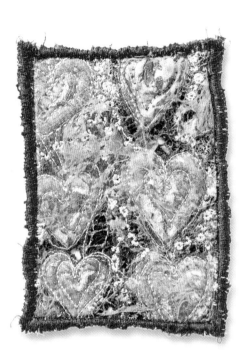
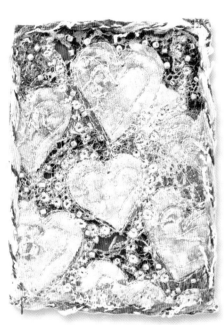

These ATCs will amaze and delight fellow swappers. With this project, you can practice free-motion embroidery skills while dabbling with stamping and bonding techniques.

RUBBERSTAMPING THE HAND-DYED FABRICS

To make the hand-dyed fabric heart motifs more complex and interesting, we're going to first rubberstamp imagery on the fabric. For this technique, I stick to rubberstamps with abstract, geometric images or text.

1   Dip a foam brush into a small amount of metallic paint and dab evenly onto a rubber-stamp. Press the rubber stamp onto a 9" × 12" (22.9 × 30.5 cm) hand-dyed fabric piece.

2   Repeat with additional rubberstamps and paints. Experiment by layering and over-lapping the images. *(Sample 1)*

3   When done, make sure to rinse the metallic paint off of your rubberstamp; otherwise your stamp will be ruined.

SAMPLE 1

FOILING ON FABRIC

To add further metallic shimmer, try using foils. *(Sample 2)*

SAMPLE 3

SAMPLE 2

1 Apply an even amount of foil glue with a foam brush to a rubberstamp and press the stamp onto the hand-dyed fabric. Stamp several impressions with glue on various parts of the fabric. Allow the glue to dry fully (about 20 to 30 minutes). Remember to wash the glue off your rubberstamp before it dries.

2 When the glue is completely dry on the fabric, place a sheet of metallic foil, *shiny side up,* on top of the glued design.

3 Burnish with a bone folder or rub the area with your fingernail.

FUSING THE FABRIC

1 Fuse the back of the hand-dyed fabric to fusible webbing, such as WonderUnder, and peel away the release paper from the fusible webbing.

> **NOTE:** This step may be done prior to stamping the hand-dyed fabric.

2 Cut fabric into simple or geometric shapes. You can choose hearts, triangles, circles, squares, and so on.

3 Fuse the geometric shapes to the black craft felt. *(Samples 4 and 5)*

SAMPLE 4

SAMPLE 5

SANDWICHING AND BONDING FIBERS

1   Snip various threads and yarns and randomly place them on top of the felt.

2   Sprinkle tiny snippets of fusible webbing or a very small amount of Bo-Nash over the thread and yarn snippets. Place a chiffon scarf on top of the felt and thread snippets.

3   Place a piece of parchment paper on top of the chiffon scarf and press. (Parchment paper protects your iron from becoming tacky from the fusible webbing.) Set the iron to the wool/cotton setting and iron the chiffon, snippets, and other bits to the felt. The fusible webbing is holding the sandwich together until it is free-motion stitched, so there may be loose bits of fabrics on top.

4   Using variegated threads, free-motion stitch around the shapes. In the examples shown, I used free-motion stitching for the hearts and accented them with an embroidered floral stitch design.

5   In a well-ventilated area or outside, take a heat gun and place it 4" to 6" (10.2 to 15.2 cm) away from your fabric. "Zap" the sandwiched piece (felt, chiffon, thread bits, heart shapes) for a few seconds in different areas, watching closely to see if bits of the chiffon are shriveling away. Do not burn all the chiffon away, but simply create holes to reveal the brighter hues below.

6   Cut the felt piece into 2.5" × 3.5" (6.4 × 8.9 cm) ATCs.

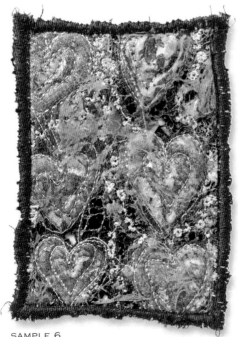

SAMPLE 6

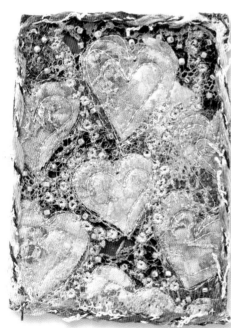

SAMPLE 7

7 Glue a decorative trim around each ATC with fabric glue.

8 When the glue is dry, you can leave the trim as is or zigzag-stitch over the trim. *(Samples 6 and 7)*

9 Cut a piece of cardstock trimmed to size and glue to the back of each trading card. Sign and date your ATCs.

Another Option: You can create a lacier effect by completely burning away the craft felt. In these two examples, I burned away most of the felt, then appliquéd the resulting designs onto mulberry bark. *(Samples 8 and 9)*

TRADING YOUR ATCs:

If you can't rally your local friends to participate in an ATC trade, there are many organized ATC groups and swaps on the Internet. Simply go to Yahoogroups.com and enter "Artist Trading Cards" in the search field. You'll find a number of groups that are swapping paper, fabric, and mixed-media ATCs, some with specific themes throughout the year. Have fun!

SAMPLE 8

SAMPLE 9

0200   0498   0685

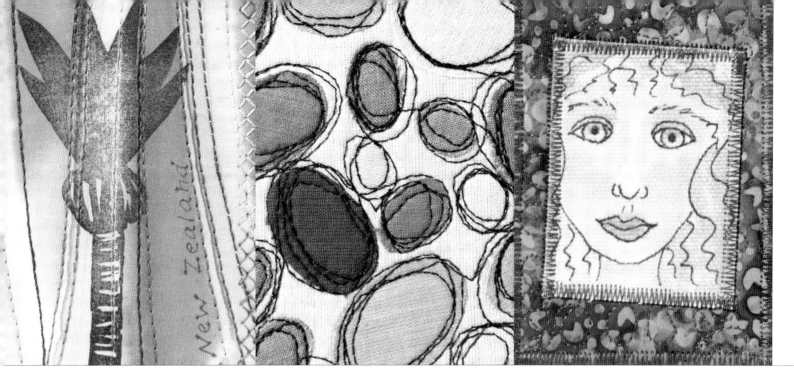

0748   0877   0344

0001   0002   0003

0004   0005

0001   0002   0003   0004   0005

ARTIST
Raine Klover

0006

Nothing turns 'em on like a little Parmesan.

0007

CROWNING GLORY

WEARING A HALO CAN GIVE YOU A HEADACHE AFTER A WHILE

0008

"I'm a real bear when my hairdresser is out of town."

Stalker

0009

Birds of a Feather Flock Together

0010

0006 0007 0008 0009 0010

ARTIST
Ruth Steinhagen

0011   0012   0013

0014   0015

OO11   OO12   OO13   OO14   OO15

ARTIST
Sandra L. Baker

0016

0017

0018

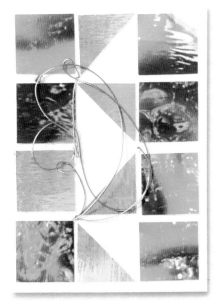

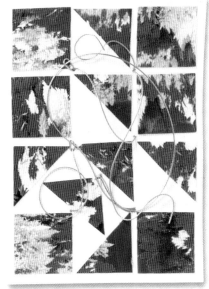

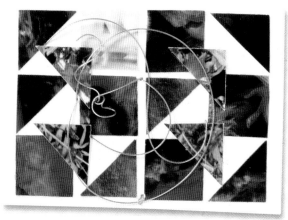

0019

0020

0016   0017   0018   0019   0020

ARTIST
Barbara Estevez

0021

0022

0023

0024

0025

0021   0022   0023   0024   0025

ARTIST
Lynne Croswell

0026

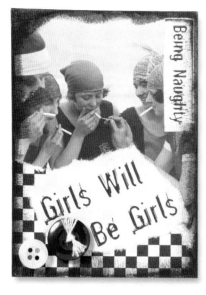

0027

0028

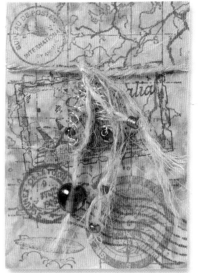

0029

0030

0026   0027   0028   0029   0030

ARTIST
Tami Shires

0031

0032

0033

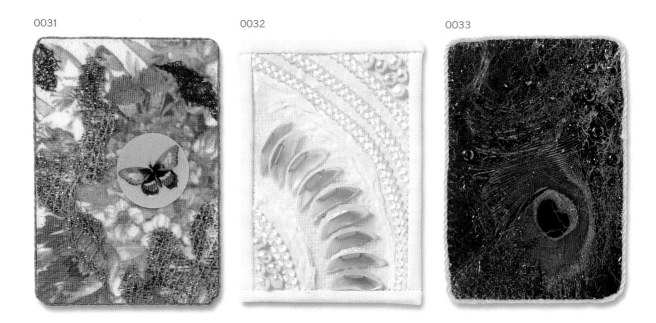

0031   0032   0033

ARTIST
Sherry Boram

0034

0035

0034 0035

ARTIST
Sherry Boram

0036

0037

0038

0036   0037   0038

ARTIST
Gayle Alstrom

0039

0040

0039   0040

ARTIST
Gayle Alstrom

0041

0042

0043

0044

0045

0041   0042   0043   0044   0045

ARTIST
Judithann Illingworth

0046

0047

0048

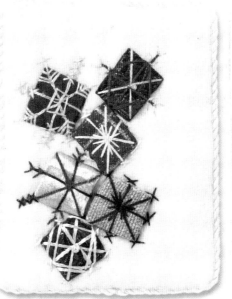

Art Embroidery

0049

0050

0046 0047 0048 0049 0050

ARTIST
Evelyn N. Elliott

0051

0052

0053

0054

0055

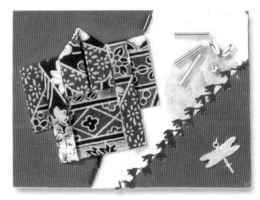

0051   0052   0053   0054   0055

ARTIST
Dorothy Debosik

0056

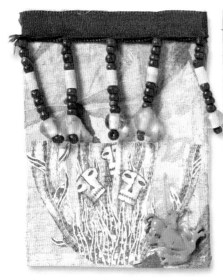

0057

0058

0059

0060

0056   0057   0058   0059   0060

ARTIST
Debbie McEllenborough

0061

0062

0063

0064

0065

0061   0062   0063   0064   0065

ARTIST
Cynthia A. Oberg

0066

0067

0068

0069

0070

0066   0067   0068   0069   0070

ARTIST
Patty Miller

0071

0072

0073

0074

0075

0071   0072   0073   0074   0075

ARTIST
Saramae Ouellette

0076   0077   0078

0079   0080

0076   0077   0078   0079   0080

ARTIST
Jill Booker

0081

0082

0083

0081   0082   0083

ARTIST
Jean K. Brown

0084

0085

0084 0085

ARTIST
Jean K. Brown

0086

0087

0088

0086   0087   0088

ARTIST
Susie Perrott

0089

0090

0089 0090

ARTIST
Susie Perrott

0091

0092

0093

0094

0095

0091   0092   0093   0094   0095

ARTIST
Valerie Lasure

0096

0097

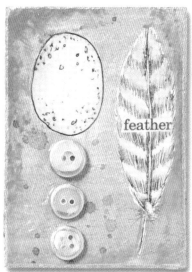

0098

0099

0100

0096   0097   0098   0099   0100

ARTIST
Kelli Perkins

0101

0102

0103

0104

0105

0101   0102   0103   0104   0105

ARTIST
Ruth Wichmann

0106

0107

0108

0109

0110

0106   0107   0108   0109   0110

ARTIST
Ruth Wichmann

O111 O112 O113 O114 O115

ARTIST
Patti Gramza

0116

0117

Be tactful:

OR NOT

0118

6   6

You should be able to undertake and complete anything.

You are deeply atta...our family and...

FAMILY & D...

0119

27

0120

0116   0117   0118   0119   0120

ARTIST
Leslie Agnello-Dean

0121   0122   0123   0124   0125

ARTIST
Cristal Marie Wooten

0126 0127 0128

0129 0130

0126 0127 0128 0129 0130

ARTIST
Pat Jennings

0131 0132 0133

0134 0135

0131 0132 0133 0134 0135

ARTIST
Judy W. Colpack

0136

0137

0138

0139

0140

0136   0137   0138   0139   0140

ARTIST
Mary Veronica Major

0141

0142

0143

0144

0145

0141 0142 0143 0144 0145

ARTIST
Sue Giduck

0146

0147

0148

0149

0150

0146   0147   0148   0149   0150

ARTIST
Susan Leahy

0151

0152

0153

0154

0155

0151 0152 0153 0154 0155

ARTIST
Laura Melohn

0156

0157

0158

0159

0160

0156   0157   0158   0159   0160

ARTIST
Lisa Mallette

0161

0162

0163

0164

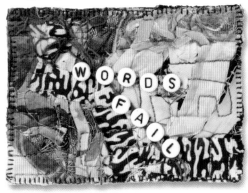

0165

0161   0162   0163   0164   0165

ARTIST
Carol Moore

0167

0166

0169

0168

0170

0166   0167   0168   0169   0170

ARTIST
Jennifer Raetz

0171

0172

0173

0174

0175

0171   0172   0173   0174   0175

ARTIST
Sara Kaetzer

0176   0177   0178

Where there is love there is life Mahatma Gandhi

Beauty is not caused. It is.
                              Emily Dickinson

0179

0180

0176   0177   0178   0179   0180

ARTIST
Mary L. Eischen

0181

0182

0183

0181   0182   0183

ARTIST
Mary Fisher

0184

0185

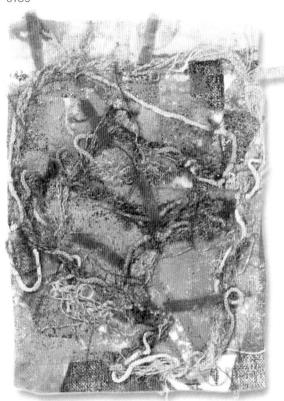

0184 0185

ARTIST
Mary Fisher

0186

0187

0186   0187

ARTIST
Kim Boehm

0188

0189

0190

0188 0189 0190

ARTIST
Kim Boehm

0191   0192   0193

0194   0195

0191   0192   0193   0194   0195

ARTIST
Linda C. Gillespie

0196

0197

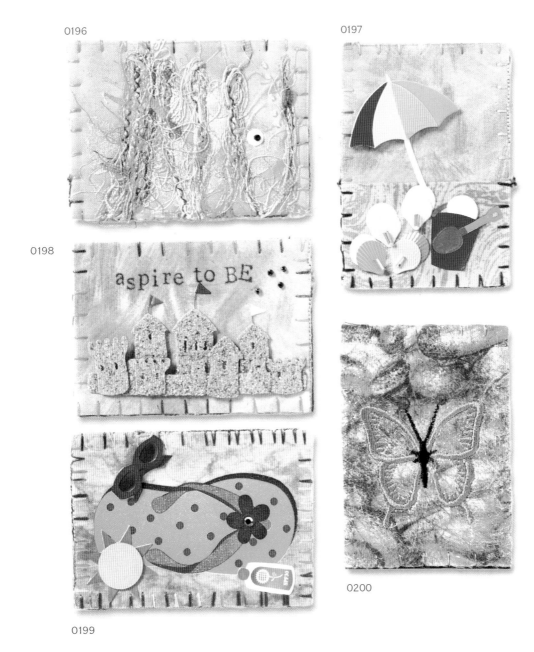

0198

0199

0200

0196   0197   0198   0199   0200

ARTIST
Juanita Olson

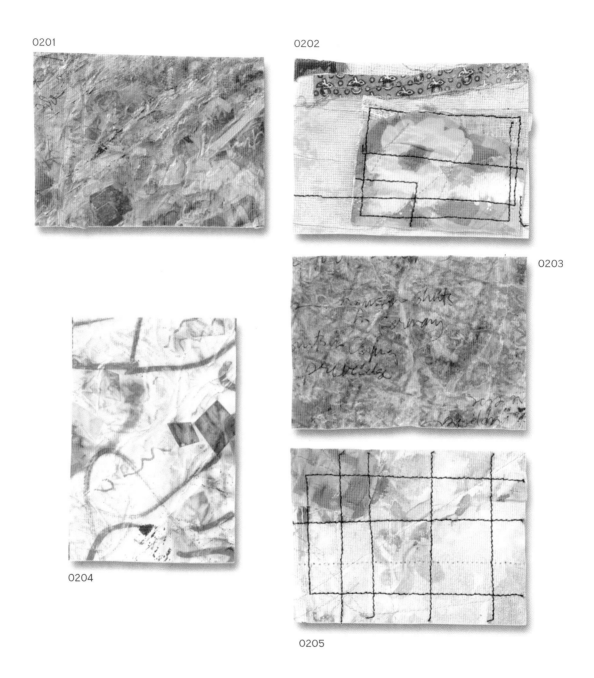

0201

0202

0203

0204

0205

0201   0202   0203   0204   0205

ARTIST
Leslee Nelson

0206   0207   0208

0209   0210

0206 0207 0208 0209 0210

ARTIST
Bonnie J. Wedge

0211   0212   0213   0214   0215

ARTIST
LeVoy Francisco

0216
0217
0218

0219
0220

0216 0217 0218   0219   0220

ARTIST
Virginia A. Spiegel

0221

0222

0223

0224

0225

0221   0222   0223   0224   0225

ARTIST
Connie McDowell

0226

0227

0228

0229

0230

0226　0227　0228　0229　0230

ARTIST
Camille Webb

0231

0232

0233

0234

0235

0231   0232   0233   0234   0235

ARTIST
Jody Cull

0236

0237

0238

0239

0240

0236   0237   0238   0239   0240

ARTIST
Bonnie Ouellette

0241

0242

0243

0244

0245

0241   0242   0243   0244   0245

ARTIST
Julie Valkanet

0246

0247

0248

0249

0250

0246   0247   0248   0249   0250

ARTIST
Carolyn M. Brady

0251

0252

0253

0254

0255

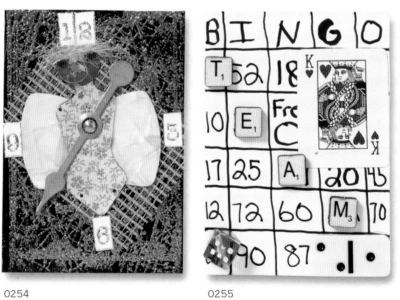

0251   0252   0253   0254   0255

ARTIST
Christina Nelson

0256

0257

0258

0259

0260

0256   0257   0258   0259   0260

ARTIST
Jane E. Maley

0261

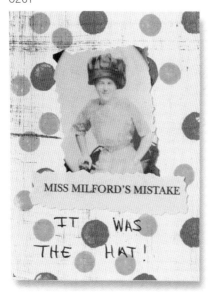

0262

0263

0264

0265

0261   0262   0263   0264   0265

ARTIST
Laura Duet

0266

0267

0268

0269

0270

0266   0267   0268   0269   0270

ARTIST
Anne Motta

0271

0272

0271   0272

ARTIST
JoAnn Johnsey

0273

0274

0275

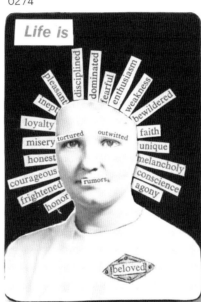

0273 0274 0275

ARTIST
JoAnn Johnsey

0276

0277

0276 0277

ARTIST
Karen Shellnut

0278

0279

0280

0278 0279 0280

ARTIST
Karen Shellnut

0281

0282

0283

0284

0285

0281   0282   0283   0284   0285

ARTIST
Kari Bauer

0286   0287   0288   0289   0290

ARTIST
Kathleen Bell

0291

0292

0293

0294

0295

0291   0292   0293   0294   0295

ARTIST
Beatriz Goodpasture

0296

0297

Time began in a Garden.....

0298

Imagination   is the

Eye

of the

Soul

0299

ENVIRONS OF PARIS

travels

"My Dear, remember, we'll always have Paris!"

CHAMBRE DES

0300

0296   0297   0298   0299   0300

ARTIST
Evalyn Gust

0301

0302

0303

0304

0305

0301 0302 0303 0304 0305

ARTIST
Orianna Abels

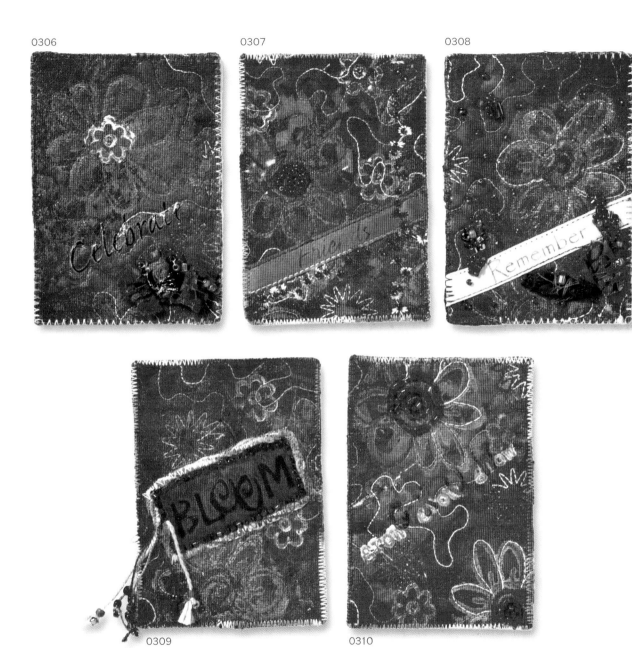

0306

0307

0308

0309

0310

0306   0307   0308   0309   0310

ARTIST
Suanne Reed

0311 0312 0313

0314 0315

0311 0312 0313 0314 0315

ARTIST
Kathy Downie

0316　　0317　　0318

0319　　0320

ARTIST
Mary Kroetsch

0321

0322

0323

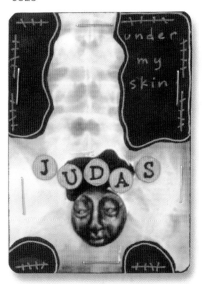

0324

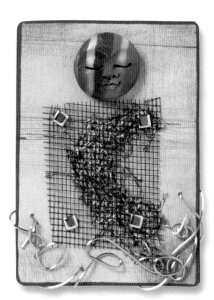

0325

0321 0322 0323 0324 0325

ARTIST
Lynn Krawczyk

0326

0327

0328

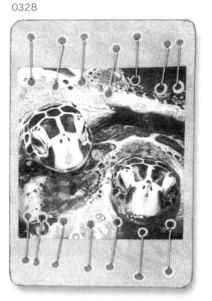

0329

0330

0326   0327   0328   0329   0330

ARTIST
Jill Hamilton-Krawczyk

0331

0332

0333

0334

0335

0331   0332   0333   0334   0335

ARTIST
Kathi Pecor

0336

0337

0338

0339

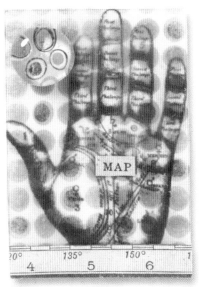
0340

0336   0337   0338   0339   0340

ARTIST
Vesna Radivojevic

0341

0342

0343

0344

0345

0341   0342   0343   0344   0345

ARTIST
Terri Stegmiller

0346

0347

0348

0349

0350

0346   0347   0348   0349   0350

ARTIST
Lynne Dubriwny

0351

0352

0353

0351 0352 0353

ARTIST
Joni King

0354

0355

0354 0355

ARTIST
Joni King

0356

0357

0356 0357

ARTIST
Darlene Wilkinson

0358

0359

0360

0358 0359 0360

ARTIST
Darlene Wilkinson

0361

0362

0363

0364

0365

0361   0362   0363   0364   0365

ARTIST
Catherine J. Wegner

0366

0367

0368

CIRQUE DU SOLEIL

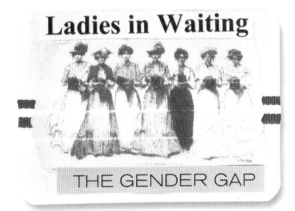

0369

0370

0366 0367 0368 0369 0370

ARTIST
Clare Lacey Gilliland

0371

0372

0373

0374

0375

0371   0372   0373   0374   0375

ARTIST
Janice Nastasi

0376   0377   0378

0379   0380

0376   0377   0378   0379   0380

ARTIST
Arlene Jarret

ARTIST
Michelle M. May

0381

0382

0383

0384

0385

O381   O382   O383   O384   O385

ARTIST
Heidi Horner

ARTIST
Michelle Caldwell

0386

0387

0388

0389

0390

0386   0387

0388

0389   0390

ARTIST
Pam Bell

ARTIST
Denise A.
Buchwalter-Losczyk

ARTIST
Pam Bell

0391

0392

0393

0394

0395

0391 0392 0393 0394 0395

ARTIST
Cindy Trobaugh

0396

0397

0398

0399

0400

0396

ARTIST
Betsy Peska

0397

ARTIST
Pat Pasquini

0398   0399   0400

ARTIST
Betsy Peska

0401

0402

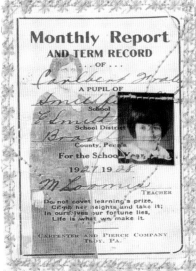

0403

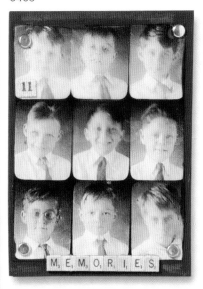

0404

0405

0401   0402   0403   0404   0405

ARTIST
Sylvia Luna/Silver Moon

0406

0407

0408

0409

0410

0406   0407   0408   0409   0410

ARTIST
Patricia Sayre McCoy

0411

0412
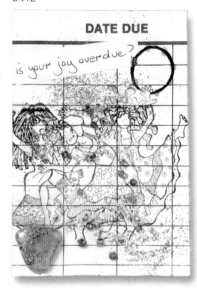

0413

0414

0415

0411   0412   0413   0414   0415

ARTIST
Marilyn Rock

ARTIST
Lynne Bright,
Tsatskeh Queen

ARTIST
Marilyn Rock

0416

0417

0418

0419

0420

0416   0417   0418   0419   0420

ARTIST
Marna Bennett

ARTIST
Linda Platt

0421

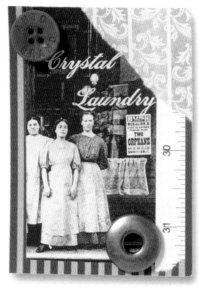

0422

0423

0424

0425

0421

ARTIST
Jill Lundstrom

0422

ARTIST
Maxine Carlstedt

0423 0424 0425

ARTIST
Jill Lundstrom

0426

0427

0428

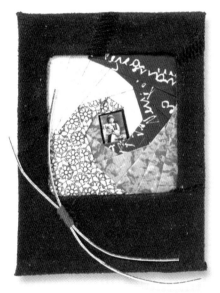

0429

0430

0426 0427 0428 0429   0430

ARTIST
Regina Portscheller

ARTIST
Bonnie Sabel

0431

0432

0433

0434

0435

0431 0432

ARTIST
Jo-Ann Foss

0433

ARTIST
Meena Schaldenbrand

0434 0435

ARTIST
Jo-Ann Foss

0436

0437

0438

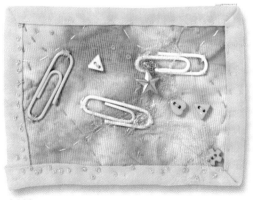

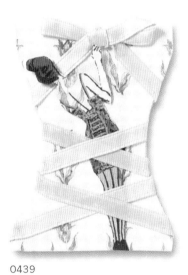

0439

0440

0436   0437   0438   0439   0440

ARTIST
McLeod Skinner

ARTIST
Cathy Lewton

0441

0442

0443

0444

0445

0441   0442   0443   0444   0445

ARTIST
Judi Wellnitz

ARTIST
Jeanne Strater

0446

0447

0448

0449

0450

0446   0447   0448   0449   0450

ARTIST
Joyce R. Hartley

ARTIST
Sharon Neth

0451

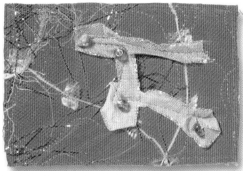

0452

0453

0454

0455

0451

ARTIST
Cheri Searles

0452

ARTIST
Maggie Hannigan

0453

ARTIST
Cheri Searles

0454

ARTIST
Kathie Serlet

0455

ARTIST
Maggie Hannigan

0456

0457

0458

0459

0460

0456   0457   0458   0459   0460

ARTIST
Adele F. Tyson

ARTIST
Cathy Baumgartner

0461

0462

0463

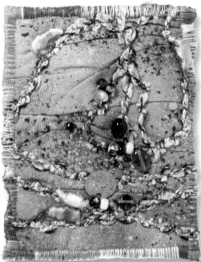

0464

0465

0461 0462 0463   0464 0465

ARTIST
Lauren Teubner

ARTIST
Ralph Beney

0466

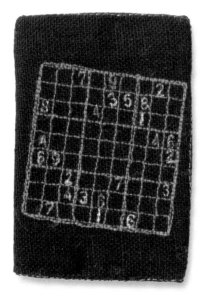

0467

0468

the mothers of families....

us philosophy.
the earth and sun and f
riches

the moon and the stars

0469

0470

0466   0467   0468   0469   0470

ARTIST
patsy monk

ARTIST
Phoebe H. Guider

0471

0472

0473

0474

0475

0471   0472   0473   0474   0475

ARTIST
Antje van Daalen

ARTIST
Elaine Bouska

0476

0477

0478

0479

0480

0476

ARTIST
Carol Hanson

0477   0478

ARTIST
Jolene Graham

0479

ARTIST
Carol Hanson

0480

ARTIST
Jolene Graham

0481

0482

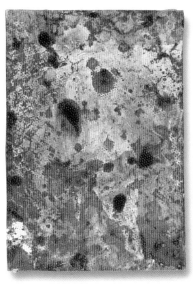

0483

0484

0485

0481   0482   0483   0484   0485

ARTIST
Mary L. Warner

ARTIST
Ann Carneal

0486

0487

0488

0489

0490

0486 0487

0488 0489 0490

ARTIST
Carol K. Boyer

ARTIST
Patti Flasch

0491

0492

0493

0494

0495

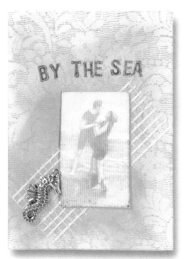

0491	0492	0493	0494	0495
ARTIST	ARTIST	ARTIST		ARTIST
Jane Melohn	Carolyn Stobba-Wiley	Jane Melohn		Mary Pendergrass

0496

0497

0498

0499

0500

0496   0497   0498   0499   0500

ARTIST
Emmy Geppert

ARTIST
Jo Denton Bryant

0501   0502   0503

0504   0505

0501 0502 0503   0504 0505

ARTIST
Karylee Doubiago

ARTIST
Jenny Huffman/granniej

0506

0507

0508

0509

0510

0506 0507   0508 0509 0510

ARTIST
Heather F. Fillman

ARTIST
Carole V. Tyson

0511

0512

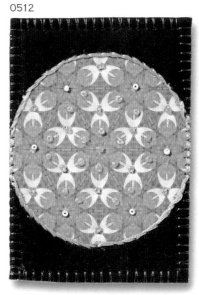

0513

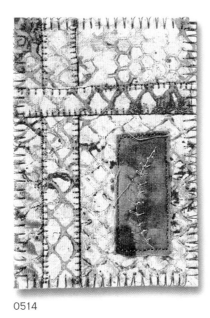

0514

0515

0511   0512   0513   0514   0515

ARTIST
Peggy Schroder

0516

0517

0518

0519

0520

0516 0517 0518

ARTIST
Jane Kirkham

0519

ARTIST
Barbara Lynne

0520

ARTIST
Jane Kirkham

0521

0522

0523

0524

0525

0521   0522   0523   0524   0525

ARTIST
Nancy Kaschmitter

ARTIST
Char DeRouin

0526

0527

0528

OFFL RULES
D GAMES

TIL SOMEONE

LOSES AN EYE

inspire

0529

art saves lives

IN HER EYES

SHE SAID WITH LOVE

0530

0526   0527   0528   0529   0530

ARTIST
Patti Hodder

ARTIST
Lori Gesing

0531

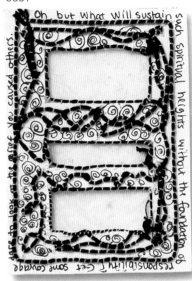

0532

swallowed parts of words.

0533

0534

for a change

0535

0531 0532 0533   0534 0535

ARTIST
Betsy Zmuda Swanson

ARTIST
Monica Dase

0536

0537

0538

0539

0540

0536

ARTIST
Jan Lewis

0537

ARTIST
Kutras Patterson

0538

ARTIST
Christine Smith

0539

ARTIST
Paula Guidry

0540

ARTIST
Christine Smith

0541

0542

0543

0544

0545

0541   0542   0543   0544   0545

ARTIST
Sandy Gordon

0546

0547

0548

0549

0550

0546   0547   0548

ARTIST
Louise Lucero

0549

ARTIST
Janet Pray

0550

ARTIST
Louise Lucero

0551

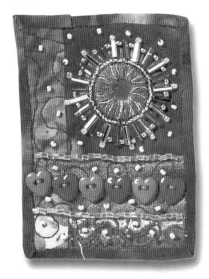

0552

0553

0554

0555

0551

ARTIST
Rachel Bastien

0552

ARTIST
Etta McFarland

0553

ARTIST
Betsy Tsukadu

0554

ARTIST
Lauren Vlcek

0555

ARTIST
Bette Fraser

0556

0557

0558

0559

0560

0556	0557	0558	0559	0560
ARTIST	**ARTIST**	**ARTIST**	**ARTIST**	**ARTIST**
Marion Coleman	Susan Bieker	Diane Camp	Anita Johnson	Sara Devern

0561

0562

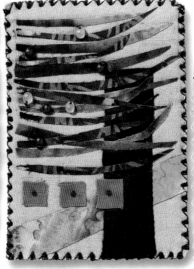

0563

0564

0565

0561

ARTIST
Julie Gausvik

0562

ARTIST
Karyn Lynam Cook

0563

ARTIST
Kathy Averett

0564

ARTIST
Mary Stanley

0565

ARTIST
Lucy Jean Smith

0566
0567
0568

0569
0570

0566

ARTIST
Tina Ritchie

0567

ARTIST
Lynne Ciacco

0568

ARTIST
Melanie Borne

0569

ARTIST
Patricia Eaton

0570

ARTIST
Dawn Browning

0571

0572

0573

0574

0575

0571
ARTIST
Debbie A. Linn

0572
ARTIST
Vivian Cavarra

0573
ARTIST
Jaime Fingal

0574
ARTIST
Chris Hardy

0575
ARTIST
Carolyn Flood

0576

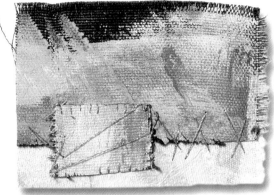

0577

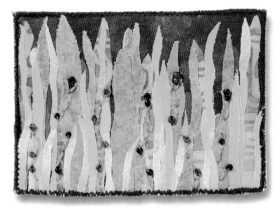

0578

0579

0580

0576	0577	0578	0579	0580
ARTIST	ARTIST	ARTIST	ARTIST	ARTIST
Gabe Cyr	Katja Stenzel	Thea Roy	Lola L. Mehlin	Nicole Menard

0581

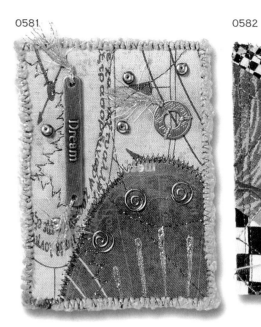

0582

0583

0584

0585

0581

ARTIST
Christine Eisenberg

0582

ARTIST
Sandra L. Baker

0583

ARTIST
Sherry Boram

0584

ARTIST
Suzanne Popalardo

0585

ARTIST
Pat Mazzarella

0586

0587

0588

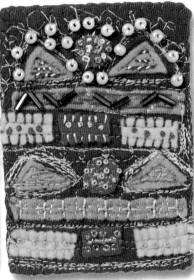

0589

0590

0586

ARTIST
Darma Redwine

0587

ARTIST
Julie Landrith

0588

ARTIST
Tina Barnes

0589

ARTIST
Marie Otero

0590

ARTIST
Irene Young

0591

0592

0593

0594

0595

0591

ARTIST
Diana Lein

0592

ARTIST
Barbara Chojnacki

0593

ARTIST
Val Thomas

0594

ARTIST
Diane Wright

0595

ARTIST
Hazel Ryder

0596

0597

0598

0599

0600

0596

ARTIST
Sarah Hester

0597

ARTIST
Judy Ireland

0598

ARTIST
Sandra L. Murphy

0599

ARTIST
Susie LaFond

0600

ARTIST
Linda Hayes

0601

0602

0603

0604

0605

0601

ARTIST
Judy Betz

0602

ARTIST
Heidi Turner

0603

ARTIST
Cynthia Morgan

0604

ARTIST
Marianna Dochtermann

0605

ARTIST
Gale Wickes

0606

0607

0608

0609

0610

0606
ARTIST
Irene Pieters-Leen

0607
ARTIST
Chris DePalma

0608
ARTIST
Steph Winn

0609
ARTIST
Diane Scheblo

0610
ARTIST
Nancy House

0611

0612

0613

0614

0615

0611

ARTIST
Lorie Rogers

0612

ARTIST
Andrea Koziol

0613

ARTIST
Sonia Grasvik

0614

ARTIST
Karen Oddo

0615

ARTIST
Laura Bailey

0616

0617

0618

0619

0620

0616

ARTIST
Regina Westmoreland

0617

ARTIST
Melissa Snyder

0618

ARTIST
Victoria Gertenbach

0619

ARTIST
Tara Travia

0620

ARTIST
Sue Giduck

0621

0622

0623

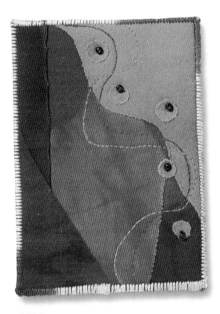

0624

0625

0621	0622	0623	0624	0625
ARTIST	ARTIST	ARTIST	ARTIST	ARTIST
Dale Rollerson	Linda C. Ross	Christine Smith	Jonna Baruffi	Anne Kaufman

0626

0627

0626 0627

ARTIST
Barbara Prince

0628

0629

0628   0629

ARTIST
Beryl Taylor

0630

0631

0632

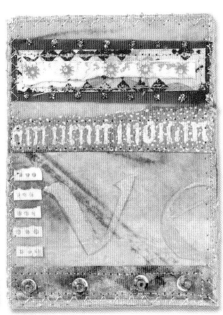

0630 0631 0632

ARTIST
Beryl Taylor

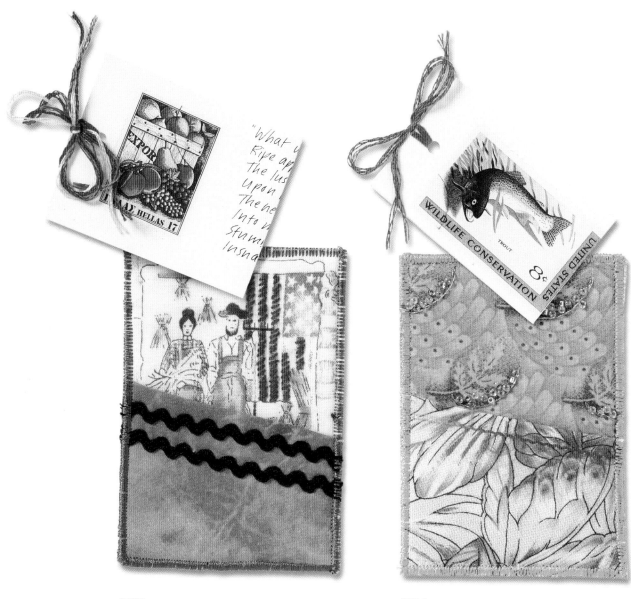

0633

0634

0633 0634

ARTIST
Lyn Kruss

0635

0636

0637

  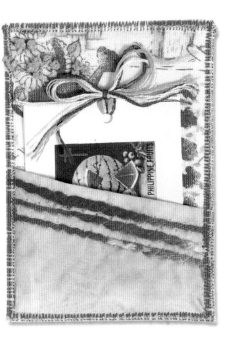

0635   0636   0637

ARTIST
Lyn Kruss

0638

0639

0638 0639

ARTIST
Wendy Richardson

0640   0641   0642

0640   0641   0642

ARTIST
Wendy Richardson

0643 0644 0645

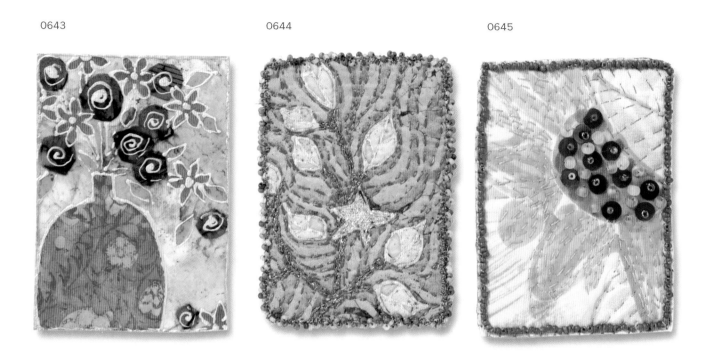

0643   0644   0645

ARTIST
Terri Haugen

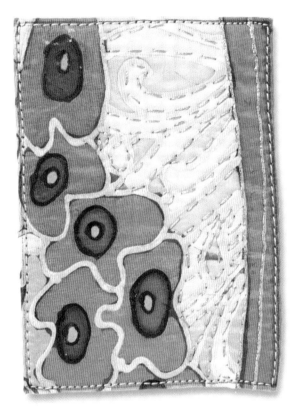

0646

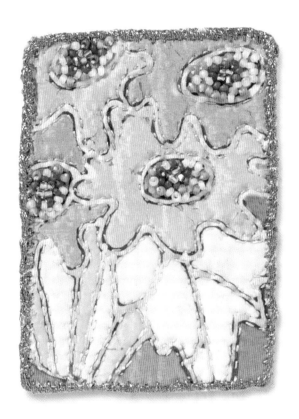

0647

0646   0647

ARTIST
Terri Haugen

0648

0649

0650

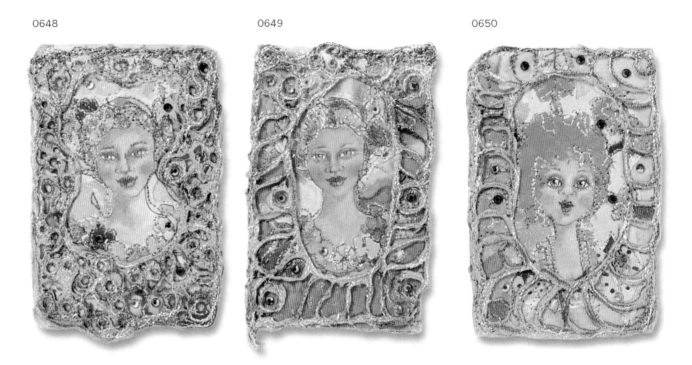

0648 0649 0650

ARTIST
Patti Medaris Culea

0651

0652

0651 0652

ARTIST
Patti Medaris Culea

0653

0654

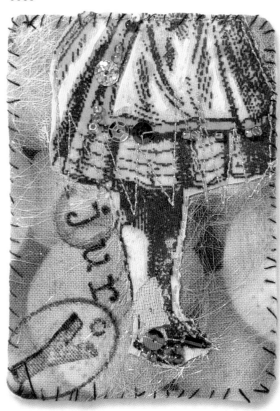

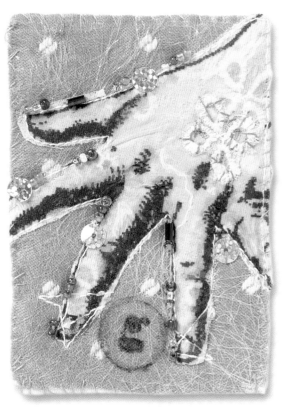

0653 0654

ARTIST
Donna Anderson

0655

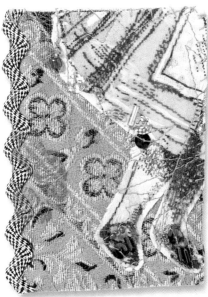

0656

0657

0655 0656 0657

ARTIST
Donna Anderson

0658

0659

0660

0658 0659 0660

ARTIST
Beth Leonadis

0661

0662

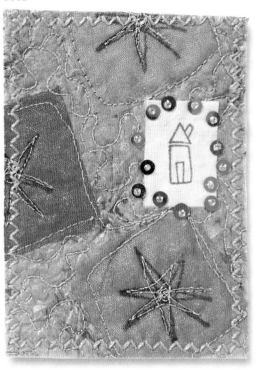

0661 0662

ARTIST
Beth Leonadis

0663

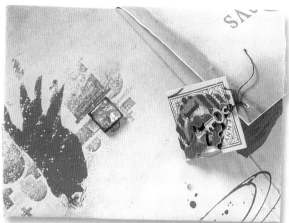

0664

0665

0663 0664 0665

ARTIST
Janet Motta

0666

0667

0668

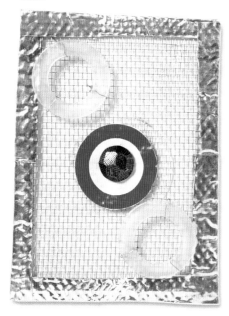

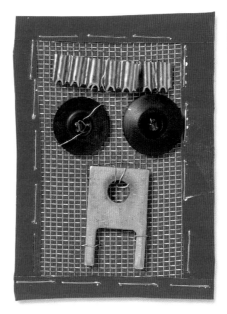

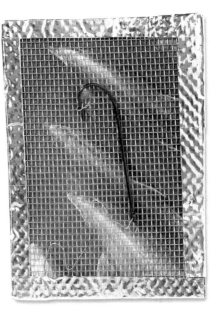

0666   0667   0668

ARTIST
Eddie Lucero

0669

0670

0671

0669   0670   0671

ARTIST
Bonnie Benson

0672

0673

0672 0673

ARTIST
Bonnie Benson

0674

0675

0676

0674

ARTIST
Dorothee Kennedy

0675   0676

ARTIST
Nadine M. Zabierek

0677

0678

0679

0677   0678   0679

ARTIST
Nadine M. Zabierek

0680 0681 0682

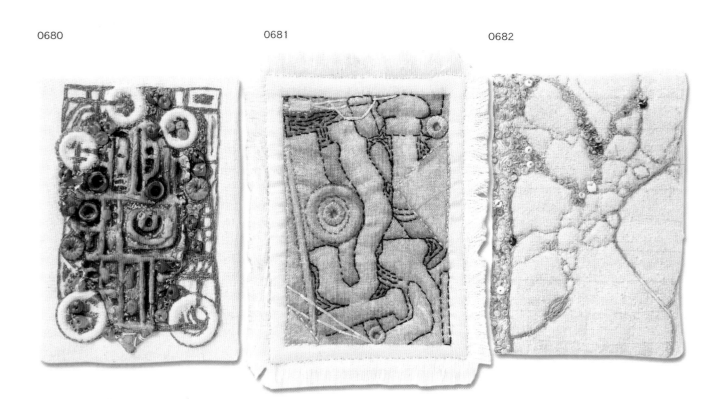

0680 0681 0682

ARTIST
Carol Penprase

0683

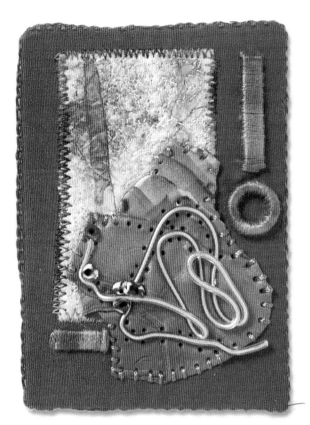

0684

0683   0684

ARTIST
Carol Penprase

0685

0686

0685   0686

ARTIST
Sharon Neth

0687

Never
Drive Faster
than your
Guardian
Angel
Can
fly

0688

0689

0687   0688   0689

ARTIST
Sharon Neth

0690

0691

0690 0691

ARTIST
Patricia Gaignat

0692

0693

0694

0692   0693   0694

ARTIST
Patricia Gaignat

0695

0696

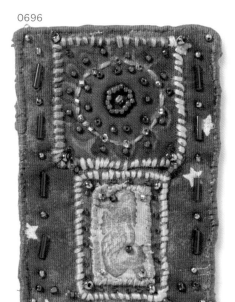

0697

0695

ARTIST
Marie Kajdasz

0696

ARTIST
Allie Thompson

0697

ARTIST
Susan Gehringer

0698

0699

0700

0698

ARTIST
Linda Rae Shea

0699

ARTIST
Theresa Kavermann

0700

ARTIST
Leanne Rogerson

0701

0702

0701

ARTIST
Diane Quinn

0702

ARTIST
Sheilah Dyson

0703

0704

0705

0703

ARTIST
Charlene Jacobsen

0704

ARTIST
Susan Hollingsworth
Becker

0705

ARTIST
Linda Ann Willis

0706

0707

0708

0706

ARTIST
Marianne Parsons

0707

ARTIST
Diane Dumas Watson

0708

ARTIST
Jeannie Moore

0709

0710

0709

ARTIST
Sue Kersey

0710

ARTIST
Suzanne Wood-Thomas

0711

0712

0713

O711

ARTIST
Lisa Martin

O712

ARTIST
Rusty Donahoo

O713

ARTIST
Meredith Price

0714

0715

0716

0714

ARTIST
Kathleen Cannon

0715

ARTIST
Suzanne Meacham

0716

ARTIST
Linda Dawson

0717

0718

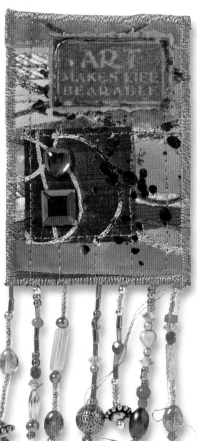

0719

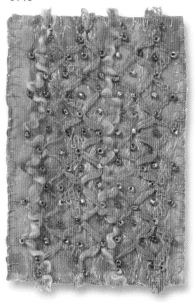

0717

ARTIST
Kimberly Pekora

0718

ARTIST
Marinda Stewart

0719

ARTIST
Carmen Holland

0720

0721

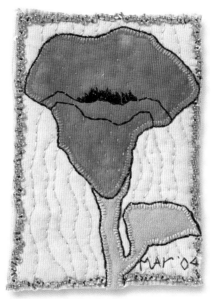

0722

0720

ARTIST
Nancy Eha

0721

ARTIST
Marin McFadden

0722

ARTIST
Vivian Milholen

0723

0724

0725

0723

ARTIST
Kath Smith

0724

ARTIST
Susan Fischer Parker

0725

ARTIST
Diane Duffield

0726

0727

0726

ARTIST
Julie Perryman

0727

ARTIST
Jill Forrey

0728

0729

0730

0728

ARTIST
Valmai Evans

0729

ARTIST
Jane Winkler

0730

ARTIST
Patti Zwick

0731

0732

0733

0731

ARTIST
Gail Holt

0732

ARTIST
Julie Wilkinson

0733

ARTIST
Kala Patterson

0734

0735

0736

0734

ARTIST
Debra Harry

0735

ARTIST
Marjorie A. DeQuincy

0736

ARTIST
Terri Kirchner

0737

0738

0737

0738

ARTIST
Karen Brockett

ARTIST
LeAnn Keller

0739

he lifted his leg
in a feline salute
to nonchalance

0740

0739

ARTIST
Nancy Karp

0740

ARTIST
Susi Bainard

0741

0742

0743

0741

ARTIST
Annika Lund

0742

ARTIST
Renée Shedivy

0743

ARTIST
Lynda Parker

0744

0745

0746

0744

ARTIST
Carmen Hilliard

0745

ARTIST
Gabrielle McIntosh

0746

ARTIST
Kay Parnaby

0747

0748

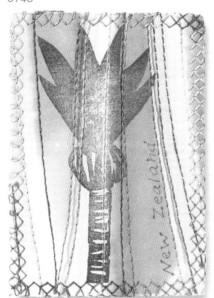

0749

0747

ARTIST
Ann Lepak

0748

ARTIST
Sheryl Sefton

0749

ARTIST
Joy Osterland

0750

0751

0752

0750

ARTIST
Catherine Lauland

0751

ARTIST
Lin Weeks

0752

ARTIST
Susan Jones

0753

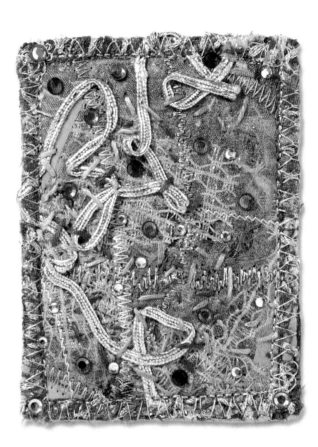

0754

0753

ARTIST
Gina Marie Cerrone

0754

ARTIST
Patricia Montgomery

0755

0756

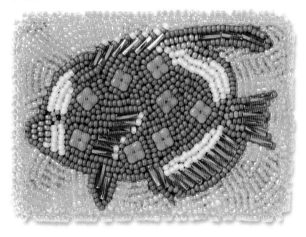

0757

0755

ARTIST
Janis Arave

0756

ARTIST
Ruth Harris

0757

ARTIST
Dianne Leatherdale Johnson

0758

0759

0760

0758

ARTIST
Phil Fisher

0759

ARTIST
Donna Akins

0760

ARTIST
Yvette Howard

0761

0762

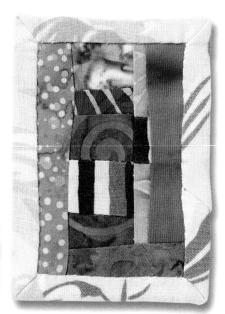

0763

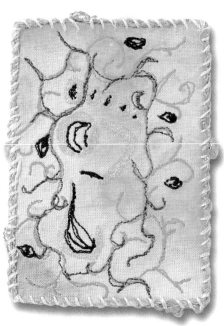

0761

ARTIST
Dolores Kinal

0762

ARTIST
Jennifer Jordan Kelley

0763

ARTIST
Katrina Kouba

0764

0765

0766

0764

ARTIST
Colette Schnieder

0765

ARTIST
Janet Ryan

0766

ARTIST
Stephanie Walker

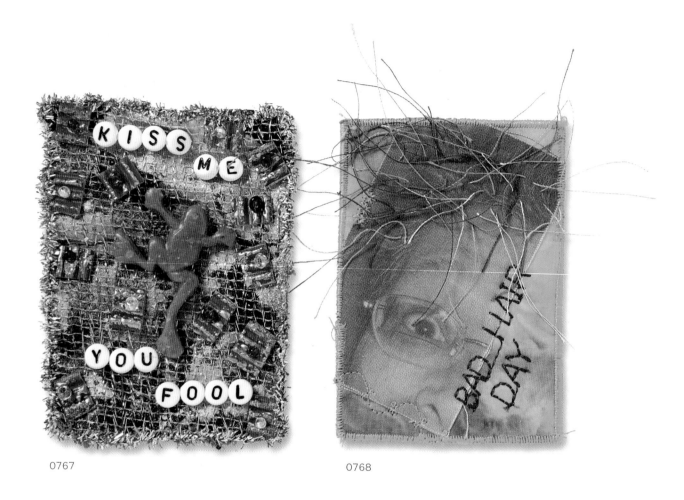

0767

0768

0767

ARTIST
Lala Ortiz

0768

ARTIST
Dolores Vitero Presley

0769

0770

0771

0769

ARTIST
Kaye Houston

0770

ARTIST
Sue Wilson

0771

ARTIST
Nancy Haarmeyer

0772

0773

0772

ARTIST
Dee Danley Brown

0773

ARTIST
Judith Kreiger

0774

0775

0774

ARTIST
j.m.scioli

0775

ARTIST
Karen Lee Carter

0776

0777

0778

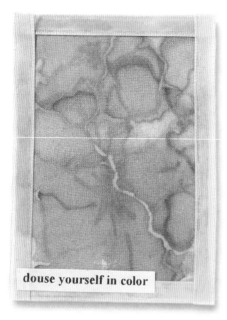

0776

ARTIST
Darlene Maciuba-Koppel

0777

ARTIST
Shirley A. Thomas

0778

ARTIST
Frances Fairchild

0779

0780

0779

ARTIST
Barbara
Rombold-Gillies

0780

ARTIST
Ava Mosley

0781

0782

0783

0781

ARTIST
Roxane Rhoads

0782

ARTIST
Margaret Pollock

0783

ARTIST
Andrea Bartsch

0784

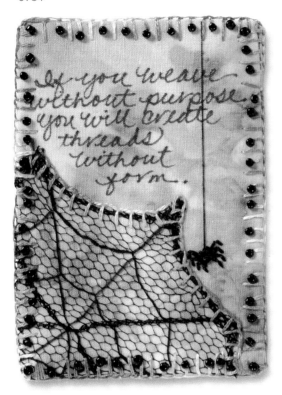

If you weave without purpose, you will create threads without form.

0785

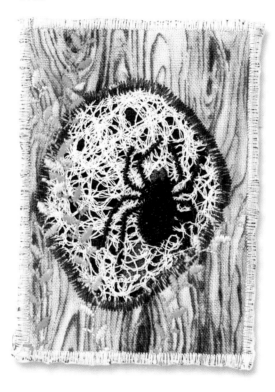

0784

ARTIST
Karyl Howard

0785

ARTIST
Becky Hoagland

0786

0787

0786

ARTIST
Shannon Spencer

0787

ARTIST
Letitia Chung

0788

0789

0790

0788

ARTIST
Karen Lonsdale

0789

ARTIST
Julz Henderson

0790

ARTIST
Kathleen Kurke

0791

0792

0791

ARTIST
Chari-Lynn Reithmeier

0792

ARTIST
Lyn Szabo

0793

0794

0793

ARTIST
Gladys Jones

0794

ARTIST
Judith Lane

0795

Berthielle duChat Renoir
1872 ~ 1884
Artiste Feline Extraordinaire

0796

0795

ARTIST
Debra Beth Bento

0796

ARTIST
Brenda Ridley

0797

0798

0799

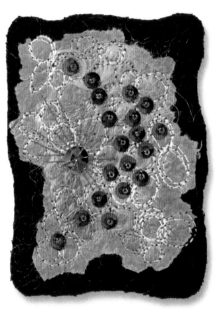

0797

ARTIST
Pam Staska

0798

ARTIST
Joan Washburn

0799

ARTIST
Sandy Jandik

0800

0801

0800

ARTIST
Paula Ellis

0801

ARTIST
Mary A. Cadwell

0802

0803

0804

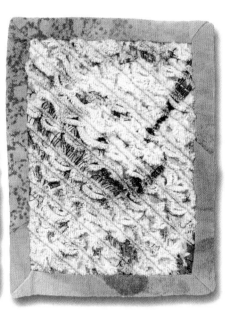

0802

ARTIST
Liz Robison

0803

ARTIST
Janice Gatti

0804

ARTIST
Gala Polk

0805

0806

0807

0805

ARTIST
Lilla LeVine

0806

ARTIST
Jenny Lucas

0807

ARTIST
Dale Ann Potter

0808

0809

0810

0808

ARTIST
Karen Goetzinger

0809

ARTIST
Joan H. Thornbury

0810

ARTIST
LeVoy Francisco

0811

0812

0813

0811

ARTIST
Rhea Kaneko

0812

ARTIST
Joyce R. Hartley

0813

ARTIST
Lyn Grenier

0814

0815

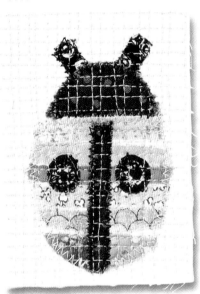

0816

0814

ARTIST
Joan Palmer

0815

ARTIST
Roseanne Pillion

0816

ARTIST
Connie Morrison

0817

0818

0817

ARTIST
Pat Davidson

0818

ARTIST
Melanie Sexton

0819

0820

0819

ARTIST
Judy Godwin

0820

ARTIST
Susan Leschke

0821

0822

0823

0821 0822 0823

ARTIST
Misty Mawn

0824

0825

0826

0824 0825 0826

ARTIST
Patricia Smith

0827

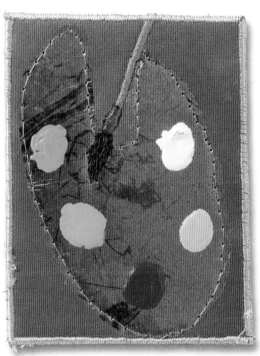

0828

0827 0828

ARTIST
Joanna van Ritbergen

0829

0830

0831

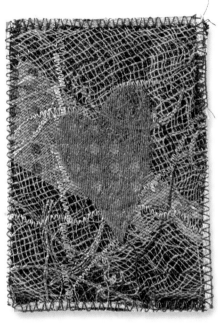

0829   0830   0831

ARTIST
Marilyn League

0832

0833

0832 0833

ARTIST
Dale Rollerson

0834

0835

0836

0834   0835   0836

ARTIST
Dale Rollerson

0837

0838

0839

0837   0838   0839

ARTIST
Tracy Stilwell

0840

0841

0840   0841

ARTIST
Tracy Stilwell

0842

0843

0842 0843

ARTIST
Debbi Crane

0844

0845

0846

0844   0845   0846

ARTIST
Debbi Crane

0847

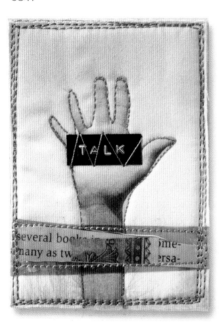

0848

0849

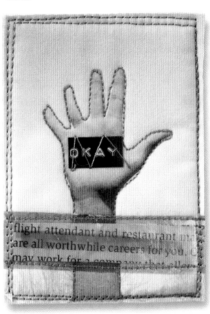

0847 0848 0849

ARTIST
Elin Waterston

0850

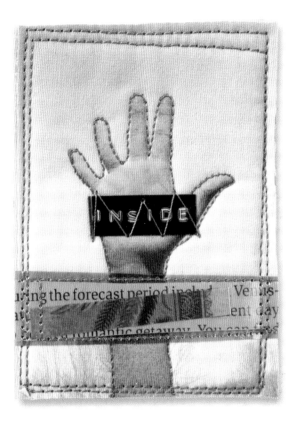

0851

0850 0851

ARTIST
Elin Waterston

0852

0853

0854

0852 0853 0854

ARTIST
Vivika Hansen DeNegre

0855

0856

0855 0856

ARTIST
Vivika Hansen DeNegre

0857

0858

0857 0858

ARTIST
Rebecca S. Cox

0859

0860

0861

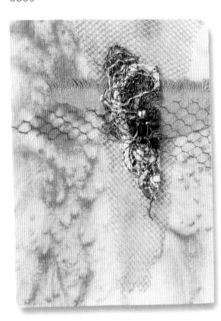

0859 0860 0861

ARTIST
Rebecca S. Cox

0862

0863

0862   0863

ARTIST
Joni King

0864

0865

0866

0864   0865   0866

ARTIST
Joni King

0867

0868

0869

0867 0868 0869

ARTIST
Pam Waller

0870

0871

0870 0871

ARTIST
Pam Waller

0872

A waist of time is the most extravagant and costly of all expense.

0873

0874

0872 0873 0874

ARTIST
Jenni Gerstle

0875

0876

0875   0876

ARTIST
Jenni Gerstle

0877

0878

0877 0878

ARTIST
Lora Disser

0879

0880

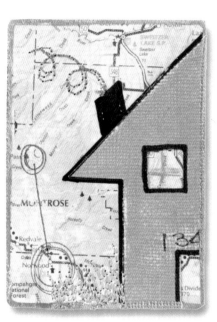

0881

0879 0880 0881

ARTIST
Lora Disser

0882

0883

0884

0882   0883   0884

ARTIST
Raine Klover

0885

0886

0885   0886

ARTIST
Raine Klover

0887

0888

0887   0888

ARTIST
Sidney S. Inch

0889   0890   0891

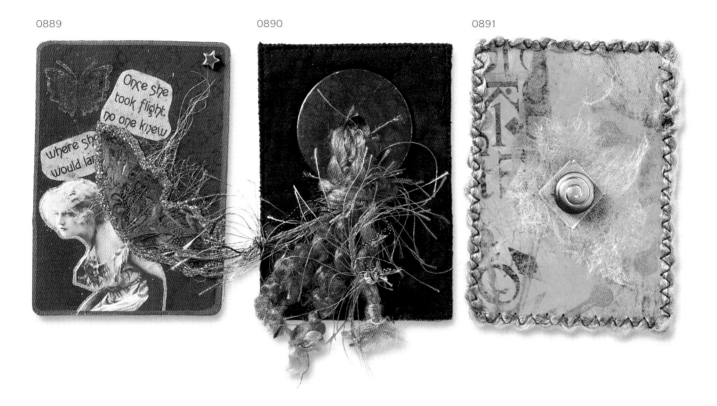

0889   0890   0891

ARTIST
Sidney S. Inch

0892

0893

0894

0892   0893   0894

ARTIST
Normajean Brevik

0895

0896

0897

0895   0896   0897

ARTIST
Erika Nelson

0898

0899

0900

0898   0899   0900

ARTIST
Kerrie Guinane

0901

0902

0903

0901 0902 0903

ARTIST
Judy Murrah

0904

0905

0906

0904 0905 0906

ARTIST
Barbara Stroup

0908

0907

0907   0908

ARTIST
Diane Ramsey

0909   0910   0911

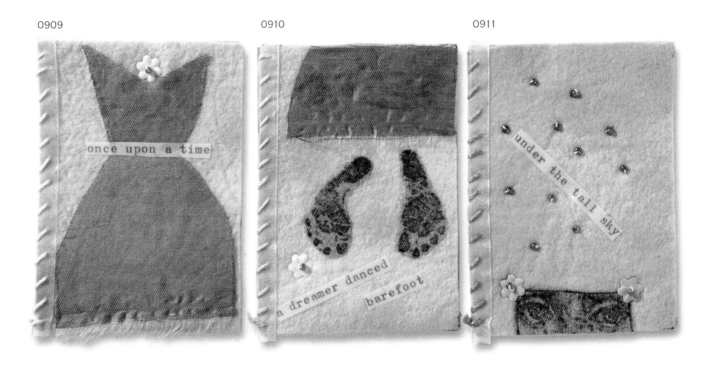

0909   0910   0911

ARTIST
Leilani Pierson

0912

0913

0912 0913

ARTIST
Leilani Pierson

0914

0915

0916

0914   0915   0916

ARTIST
Sandy Mayfield

0917

0918

0919

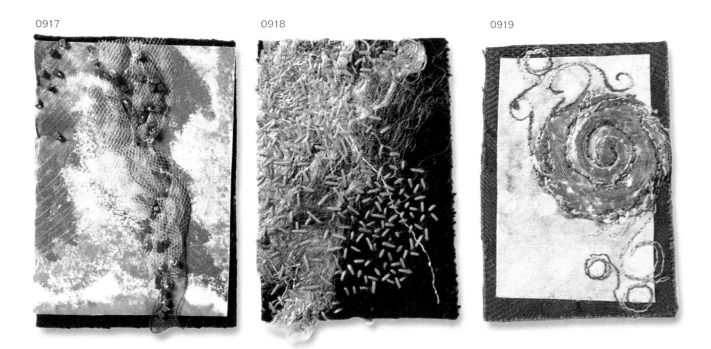

0917   0918   0919

ARTIST
Sonja Lee

0920

0921

0920   0921

ARTIST
Sioux

0922

0923

0924

0922   0923   0924

ARTIST
Laura Brandon

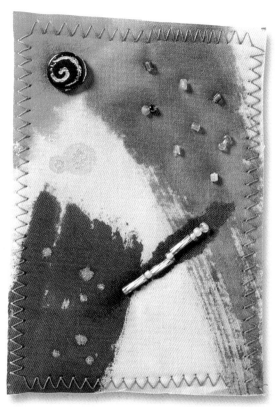

0925

0926

0925 0926

ARTIST
Karen Cross

0927

0928

0927 0928

ARTIST
Karen Cross

0929

0930

0929   0930

ARTIST
Lelainia Lloyd

0931

0932

0933

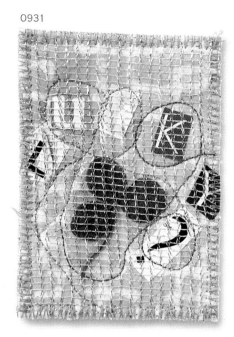

0931   0932   0933

ARTIST
Bethany Smith

0934

0935

0934 0935

ARTIST
Lynn Gallagher

0936

0937

Hot flash

0936 0937

ARTIST
Lynn Gallagher

0938

0939

0938 0939

ARTIST
Sharon Bertram

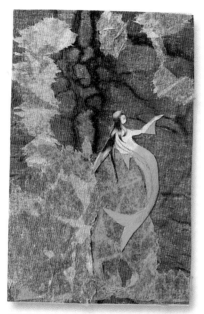

0940

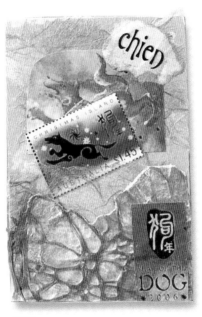

0941

0942

0940   0941   0942

ARTIST
Priscilla McGarry

0943

0944

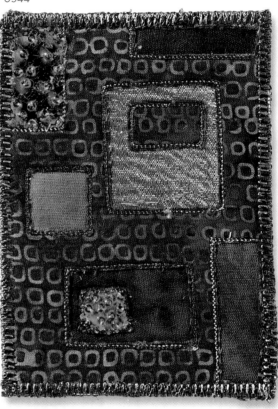

0943 0944

ARTIST
Gordana Vukovic

0945

0946

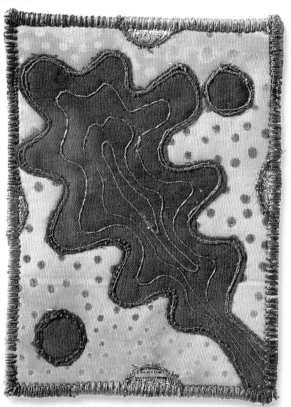

0945 0946

ARTIST
Gordana Vukovic

0947

0948

0947   0948

ARTIST
Maureen Lardie

0949

0950

0949   0950

ARTIST
Vix Lowmiller

0951

0952

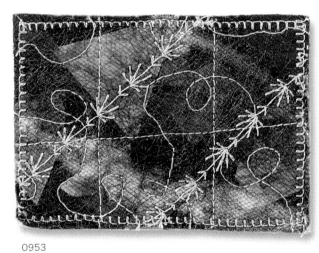

0953

0951   0952   0953

ARTIST
Brenda Manley

0954

0955

0954   0955

ARTIST
Leann Meixner

0956

0957

0956 0957

ARTIST
Jody Cull

0958

0959

0960

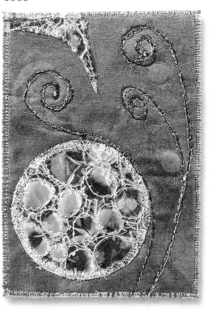

0958

ARTIST
Wendy Coyne

0959

ARTIST
Kim DeCoste

0960

ARTIST
Sandra Schnakenbowg

0961

0962

0961   0962

ARTIST
Pat Hardwick

0963

0964

0965

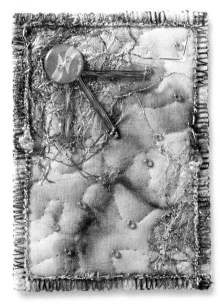

0963

ARTIST
Deborah Smith

0964

ARTIST
Ruth Ann Olson

0965

ARTIST
Darlene Maciuba Koppel

0966

0967

0968

0966   0967   0968

ARTIST
Teresa Barrett

0969

0970

0969 0970

ARTIST
Teresa Barrett

0971   0972   0973

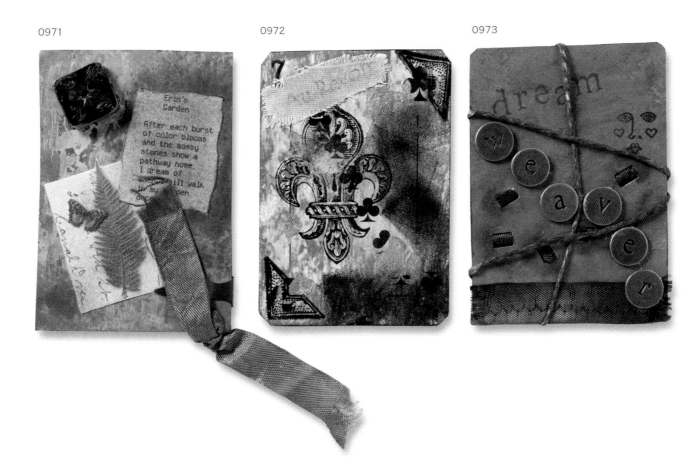

Erin's
Garden

After each burst
of color blooms
and the mossy
stones show a
pathway home.
I dream of
when I will walk
in my garden
once more.

0971 0972 0973

ARTIST
Kim Hondel

0974

0975

0976

0974

ARTIST
Jeane Walker Sliney

0975

ARTIST
Susan Barker

0976

ARTIST
Sandy Jandik

0977

0978

0979

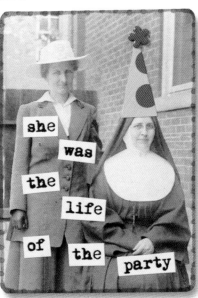

0977   0978   0979

ARTIST
Jill N. Hamilton-Krawczyk

0980

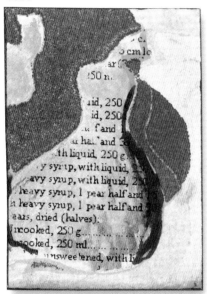

0981

0982

0980 0981 0982

ARTIST
Patricia Gaignat

0983

0984

0983

0984

ARTIST
Janet Moreland

ARTIST
Lisabeth Gutierrez

0985

0986

0985

0986

ARTIST
Zoe Enright

ARTIST
Lisa Flowers Ross

0987

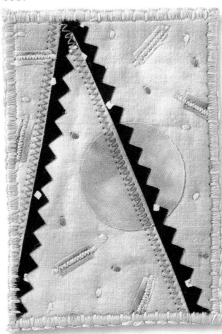

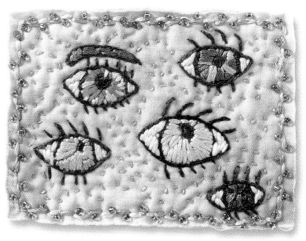

0988

0987

0988

ARTIST
Kathy Grilli

ARTIST
Becky Kelly

0989

0990

0989

ARTIST
Kari Johnson

0990

ARTIST
Viv White

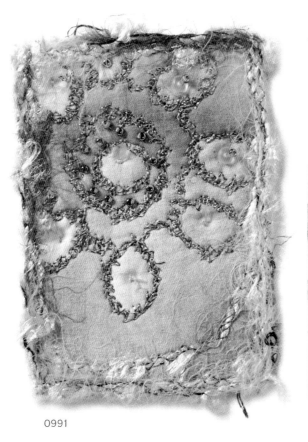

0991

0992

0991

ARTIST
Magda Clark

0992

ARTIST
Beth Mastin

0993

0994

0993

ARTIST
Carol Spader

0994

ARTIST
Mary Ann Richardson

0995

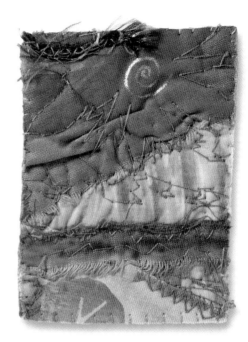

0996

0997

0995

ARTIST
Linda Sharp

0996

ARTIST
Nadine Cloutier

0997

ARTIST
Nancy Clairborne

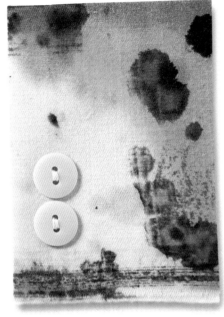

0998

0999

1000

0998

ARTIST
Vicki Neff

0999

ARTIST
Carol Morrisey

1000

ARTIST
Rhena Ferris

Designer Directory and Index

Please visit www.quarrybooks.com for complete listings of our ATC designers.

Paula Guidry
0539

Kerrie Guinane
page 5, 0898
0898–0900

Evalyn Gust
0296–0300

Lisabeth Gutierrez
0984

Nancy Haarmeyer
0771

Jill N. Hamilton-Krawczyk
page 6, 0977
0326–0330
0977–0979

Margaret Hannigan
0452, 0455

Carol Hanson
0476, 0479

Pat Hardwick
0961–0962

Chris Hardy
0574

Ruth Harris
0756

Debra Harry
0734

Joyce R. Hartley
0446–0449, 0812

Terri Haugen
0643–0647

Linda Hayes
page 7, 0600
0600

Julz Henderson
0789

Sarah Hester
0596

Carmen Hilliard
0744

Becky Hoagland
0785

Patti Hodder
0526–0527

Carmen Holland
0719

Gail Holt
0731

Kim Hondel
0971–0973

Heidi Horner
0381

Nancy House
0610

Kaye Houston
0769

Karyl Howard
0784

Yvette Howard
0760

Jenny Huffman/granniej
0504–0505

Judithann Illingworth
0041–0045

Sidney S. Inch
page 9, 0888
0887–0891

Judy K. Ireland
0597

Charlene Jacobsen
0703

Sandy Jandik
0799, 0976

Arlene Jarret
0376–0379

Pat Jennings
0126–0130

JoAnn Johnsey
0271–0275

Anita Johnson
0559

Dianne Leatherdale
Johnson
0757

Kari Johnson
0989

Gladys Jones
0793

Susan Jones
0752

Sara Kaetzer
0171–0175

Marie Kajdasz
0695

Rhea Kaneko
0811

Nancy Karp
0739

Nancy Kaschmitter
0521–0523

Anne Kaufman
0625

Theresa Kavermann
0699

LeAnn Keller
0738

Jennifer Jordan Kelley
0762

Becky Kelly
0988

Dorothee Kennedy
0674

Sue Kersey
0709

Dolores Kinal
0761

Joni King
0351–0355, 0862–0866

Terri Kirchner
0736

Jenni Kirkham
0516–0518, 0520

Raine Klover
0001–0005, 0882–0886

Katrina Kouba
0763

Andrea Koziol
0612

Lynn Krawczyk
0321–0325

Judith Kreiger
0773

Mary Kroetsch
0316–0320

Lyn Kruss
0633–0637

Kathleen Kurke
0790

Susie LaFond
0599

Julie Landrith
0587

Judith Lane
0794

Maureen Lardie
0947–0948

RESOURCES

INTERNET GROUPS FOR SWAPPING ATCS

There are several groups at Yahoogroups.com that host and discuss mixed-media and fabric ATC trades, swaps, and construction tips and tricks.

Art Trading

Cardsgroups.yahoo.com/group/ArtTradingCards/

Artisttradingcards

groups.yahoo.com/group/artisttradingcards/

ATC World

groups.yahoo.com/group/ATC_World

Fiber ATCS

groups.yahoo.com/group/FiberATC/

PUBLICATIONS

Quilting Arts Magazine and *Cloth Paper Scissors*

P.O. Box 685
23 Gleasondale Rd.
Stow, MA 01775 USA
www.quiltingartsllc.com
978.897.7750

Articles on the history of ATCs, techniques for constructing and embellishing ATCs

MATERIALS

UNITED STATES

100 Proof Press

www.100proofpress.com
740.594.2315
Rubber stamps

Acey Deucy

P.O. Box 194
Ancram, NY 12502
Rubber stamps

Alpha Stamps

www.alphastamps.com
Stamps

Anima Designs

www.animadesigns.com
Rubber stamps, ephemera

Bernina

www.bernina.com
Sewing and embroidery machines

Blumenthal Craft
Blumenthal-Lansing Company

www.buttonsplus.com
Buttons, photo fabrics, image disks

Bonnie's Best Art Tools

www.coilconnection.com
404.869.0081
Eyelet punches, eyelets, brads, other hardware

Clover

www.clover-usa.com
Appliqué pins, bias tape makers, pressing and marking tools

Coffee Break Design

www.coffeebreakdesign.com
317.290.1542
Eyelets, brads, eyelet setters, clear buttons

Contemporary Cloth

www.contemporarycloth.com
866.415.3372
Fabrics

Dharma Trading

www.dharmatrading.com
800.542.5227
Procion dye, stamps

Dick Blick

www.dickblick.com
800.828.4548
Art supplies

The DMC Corporation

www.dmc-usa.com
Embroidery threads, notions

Dover Publications

www.doverpublications.com
Clip art, copyright-free images

Dymo

www.dymo.com
800.426.7827 ext. 2
LetraTag labelmaker, fabric tapes

eQuilter

877-FABRIC-3
www.equilter.com
Fabric, notions

Fancifuls Inc.
www.fancifulsinc.com
607.849.6870
Charms, embellishments

Fire Mountain Gems
1 Fire Mountain Way
Grants Pass, OR 97526-2373
www.firemountaingems.com
Beads, charms, related supplies

Golden Paint
www.goldenpaint.com
800.959.6543
Acrylic medium

Hancocks of Paducah
3841 Hinkleville Rd.
Paducah, KY 42001
www.hancocks-paducah.com
800.845.8723
Online source for hundreds of cottons and novelty fabrics

Houston Art, Inc.
www.houstonart.com
800.272.3804
OmniGel transfer medium

Invoke Arts
1036 Chorro St.
San Luis Obispo, CA 93401
805.541.5197
www.invokearts.com
Stamps

Jacquard Paints
www.jacquardproducts.com
800.442.0455
Lumiere fabric paints

Jo-Ann Fabric & Crafts
www.joann.com
Tools, notions, fabric, craft supplies

Joggles
www.joggles.com
(Internet orders only)
Hot water-soluble fabric, Pellon, Kunin felt, fabric paints

June Tailor
www.junetailor.com
800.844.5400
Printer fabric sheets, iron-on transfer sheets

Junque
www.junque.net
Rubber stamp images and alphabets

Lonni Rossi
www.lonnirossi.com
610.896.0500
Typographic design fabrics

Ma Vinci's Reliquary
www.crafts.dm.net/mall/reliquary
Rubber stamp images and alphabets

Mantofev
www.mantofev.com
Ephemera, fabrics

Meinke Toy
www.meinketoy.com
Hot water–soluble fabric, Xpandaprint, mixed-media supplies

Michael's
www.michaels.com
Art and craft supplies

Patti's Stargazers   P. 172
www.pmcdesigns.com
858.484.5118
Dollmaking and fabric art supplies

Pearl Paint Company
www.pearlpaint.com
800.451.PEARL

Postmodern Design
postmoderndesign@aol.com
405.321.3176
Rubber stamp images, alphabets, and quotes

Quiltingarts, LLC
www.quiltingartsllc.com
866.698.6989
Magazines, books, mixed-media supplies, rubber stamps, transparencies, fibers, trims

Ranger Ink
www.rangerink.com
800.244.2211
Pigment inks, dye-based inks

St. Theresa Textile Trove
www.sttheresatextile.com
800.236.2450
Fabrics, beads, buttons

Stamp Diva
www.stampdiva.com
Rubber stamps

Stampers Anonymous
3110 Payne Ave.
Cleveland. OH 44114
800.945.3980
www.stampersanonymous.com
Rubber stamps

Thai Silks
State St. Dept. QA
Los Altos, CA 94022
www.thaisilks.com

Treasures of the Gypsy
GypsyTreasures@cs.com
505.847.0963
Exotic fabrics, appliqué trims

Turtle Press
www.turtlearts.com
Rubber stamp alphabets

Utrecht Art
6 Corporate Drive
Cranbury, NJ 08512
www.utrecht.com
609.409.8001
Paints, brushes, paper/board

Volcano Arts
www.volcanoarts.biz
209.296.6535
*Metallic rub-ons, mixed-media
supplies*

Zettiology
www.zettiology.com
*Rubber stamp images, alphabets,
and quotes*

AUSTRALIA

Bondi Road Art Supplies
179-181 Bondi Rd.
Bondi, NSW 2026
+61.02.9387.3746
www.bondiroadart.com.au
Art and craft supplies

**Eckersley's Arts, Crafts
and Imagination**
www.eckersleys.com.au
+61.1800.227.116

The Thread Studio
6 Smith St.
Perth 6000
Western Australia
www.thethreadstudio.com
+61.89227.1561
Mixed-media and fiber solutions

FRANCE

Graphigro
6e arrondissement
133, Rue de Rennes
Paris
www.graphigro.com
Art supplies

UNITED KINGDOM

ArtVanGo
www.artvango.co.uk
+44.01.438.814946

*Gesso, Japanese paper, lokta
paper, metal shim, mulberry
paper, pebeo gel, watercolor
paper, Procion Dye, Deka Dyes,
Tyvek, Xpandaprint*

Creative Crafts
11 The Square, Winchester
Hampshire WO23 9ES
www.creativecrafts.co.uk
+44.01962.856266
Crafting supplies

HobbyCraft
Stores throughout the UK
Head Office
Bournemouth, England
www.hobbycraft.co.uk
+44.01202.596100
Art and craft supplies

Impressive Images
22 Green Drive
Timperley, Altrincham
Cheshire, WA15 6JW
impressiveimages2004@
 yahoo.com
+44.0161.980.1732
Mail-order rubber stamp company

Stef Francis
www.stef-francis.co.uk
+44.0180.332.3004
*Hand-dyed threads, silk fibers,
mixed-media supplies*

Acknowledgments

First and foremost, I want to express my thanks to Mary Ann Hall—one of the smartest and kindest editors around. This project was quite an ambitious undertaking, and I'm grateful for her friendship, patience, and collaboration. What an honor to be asked to partner with Quarry Books (and her) on this project.

I'd also like to give my heartfelt thanks to fellow *Quilting Arts*, LLC editors, Barbara Delaney and Cate Prato, and also to my sister-in-law, Sally Murray, mostly because they haven't committed me to the insane asylum yet for my crazy ideas, projects, and reader challenges that often mean unexpected work for them. Thank you for enabling me!

When I first dreamed up the idea of an ATC swap between readers and our editorial team, little did I know that more than 800 of you would actually take me up on it. To all of those who submitted ATCs over the years, your little reflections of yourselves brightened our days and made our jobs that much more amusing.

Somehow I got very lucky in marrying John Bolton—intelligent, creative, hardworking, a supporter of the arts, and a firm believer in people following their dreams. Thank you for always giving loving support…and I promise that very soon, I'll bite my tongue and go a week straight without talking shop at the dinner table.

To my in-laws, Dick and Dot Bolton, you've been tireless cheerleaders all along. Ever since day one when you let me set up my Mac in the barn, you took my vision seriously. I get a lump in my throat whenever I think of how supportive you've both been to me in every respect over the years. Thanks for encouraging a girl to follow her dream. This one's for you.

—Patricia

ABOUT THE AUTHOR

PATRICIA BOLTON was introduced to art quilting and the related needle arts in 1998 when she used some Christmas money to buy her first sewing machine. Ever since she made her first stitch (a fly) and embroidered her first motif (a spider), she has been entangled in this hobby and doesn't envision herself ever breaking free. Embellished quilting and mixed-media arts have, quite literally, taken over her life—so much so that she left her doctoral program and full-time job as a special education teacher to found *Quilting Arts Magazine* in 2001. In 2004, she and her husband launched a second publication, *Cloth Paper Scissors*. When she's not attending a quilt show or mixed-media exhibit, she can be found puttering in her studio or clicking away on her keyboard in Stow, Massachusetts. She can be reached through the *Quilting Arts* website at www.quiltingartsllc.com.

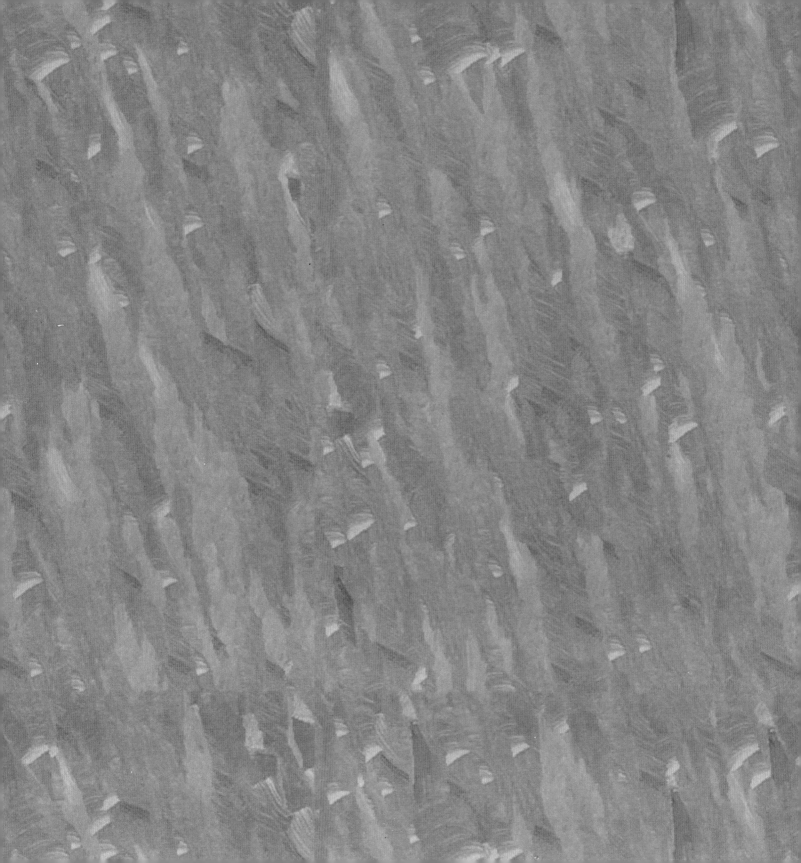